Creating places for happy humans:
Theory and design in the social age

Creating places for happy humans : Theory and design in the social age

Martin Butcher PhD

Cover illustration: Helen Butcher
Figures: Xavier Butcher
Cover design: Deb Humphreys

Typeset by BookPOD

Disclaimer
The material in this book is general comment only and neither purports nor intends to be specific advice related to any particular reader. It does not represent professional advice and should not be relied on as the basis for any decision or action on any matter that it covers. To the maximum extent permitted by law, the author and publisher disclaim all responsibility and liability to any person or entity, whether a purchaser or not, in respect to anything and of the consequences of anything done by any such person in reliance, whether in whole or in part, upon the whole or any part of the contents of this publication.

ISBN: 978-0-6488440-0-6 (pbk)

NATIONAL LIBRARY OF AUSTRALIA

A catalogue record for this book is available from the National Library of Australia

With special thanks to my wife Deb for all her support and willingness to explore new adventures, and to Bob Dick, John Gregory and David Rourke for reading drafts along the way and providing really useful insights.

Contents

Preface

This is a story about optimism and idealism. Or rather, if you happen to be a bit idealistic and wish well for the world, I want to tell an optimistic story that you, the reader, will find practical, useful and enjoyable. There is no shortage of reasons for dismay about the current state of the world – from gender equity (NOT!) to environmental catastrophe, big government to small-minded capitalists, from financial meltdown to hungry cities, there is plenty to worry about regarding our planet and all that reside on it. In this book I want to tell a hopeful story, not just because I feel that we have the potential to create a better world, but because my work over the last twenty years suggests it is also within our capacity.

I grew up in a household dedicated to good design and our family holidays were spent looking at buildings. These were an informal, continuous guided tour often accompanied by Nikolaus Pevsner's *Buildings of England* or the Michelin guide to the buildings of France. It was through these activities that I began to place buildings in context with school history lessons. This introduction was augmented later by the wonderful history of architecture lectures by Bastion Valkenburg at Kingston Polytechnic. This being the 1970s, there was still considerable emphasis on the role of the Bauhaus and the designers of the early modern movement not only as a style, but as a philosophy based on idealism and technology. I was a student at Kingston when I realised that so much of what was revered about these modern masters had somehow become lost in our everyday environment. The promise of *Unité d'habitation* had emerged as poorly designed and built public housing estates standing in windswept parking lots, or soulless shopping centres in dreary New Towns. This realisation then led to a multi-pronged search to uncover what, in today's age, would be good design? What kind of expression would embody the excitement and idealism of modernism?

One line of thought resulted in an interest in alternative and appropriate technology. This was as a response to the work of Jane Jacobs, Rachel Carson, the Club of Rome, Ernst Schumacher, Barbara Ward, and James Lovelock among others. It seemed a reasonable response to the idea of environmental sustainability. This trajectory led to both designing and building low-tech buildings in Africa and later living in an intentional community in Nimbin, Australia's most (in)famous alternative town. Whilst these experiences were interesting and informative in many ways, a critical learning was a personal understanding of how romanticism (perceiving the past as preferable to the present) is false optimism.

Another line of enquiry was through the writings of critics and theorists such as Reyner Banham and Paul Oliver, who looked at the relationship between architecture and society. I had spent hours looking through the photos in Bernard Rudofsky's *Architecture without Architects* and was quite prepared to accept that the buildings illustrated in these books have qualities that could be described as architecture. From longhouses in Papua New Guinea to igloos in the Arctic, these were indeed wonderful expressions of built form: structures that created a spatial experience that both responded to the culture and transcended what might be required for shelter alone. The difference to what was created by those heroic architects of the modern movement was that these were the expressions of an unselfconscious culture, saying 'Traditional architecture is what we do

1

around here and what we've always done around here'. These structures are an integral part of the culturally accepted norms of how society was organised. Culture and building were inextricably interwoven. It was from this perspective that I began to wonder if modern culture is just as hidebound and subject to its own shibboleths as all others.

The challenge was to reconcile the dichotomy between traditional cultures, and the traditionalism of a culture that reveres change: a culture that views technological development as a given, a culture that places considerable value on innovative products.

In thinking more about the difference between traditional cultures and modern culture I determined that there are two very different aspects to that difference. The first is the idea of change and growth, the second relates to ideas about control and choice.

Throughout the last 1000 years of history, expressions of architecture and city development have reflected an underlying dynamic, or driver, about the individual's control and choice in their everyday life. New and emerging architectural expression reflected new and emerging thought and expressions of change in society. Whilst romantic in much of its expression, the alternative movement of the 1960s and 1970s was also, at its core, about control and choice. This was loosely conveyed as 'We want to opt out of mainstream consumer society and live in a dome, build a house out of recycled car tops, convert our bicycle to a power generator. Be self-sufficient, disconnected from the mainstream.' Wherever I looked, I saw that a critical difference between traditional culture and the idea of modernity was the idea of individual control and choice. But it still left the question of what should a contemporary development practitioner actually do in today's world? To answer that question required understanding another critical component of modernity.

As well as *control and choice* being a key difference between *modern* and *traditional* cultures, there is also the idea of change and growth. In the natural environment, life is full of examples where things evolve over time from one state to another. Seeds become trees, babies become adults, caterpillars become butterflies. And when you are in a particular state, that is the state you are in. The transition is often startling to both outside observers and the entity itself. That goofy kid suddenly becomes a mature and sensible adult. The difference between caterpillar and butterfly is incomprehensible.

After designing a wide range of buildings in Africa within a philosophy of being low-tech, culturally appropriate and environmentally sustainable, I was still searching for the answer to my quest. A catalytic step was when my wife and I bought into a community title property consisting of 13 hectares of degraded pastoral land in northern New South Wales. This became a significant learning exercise that led to what might be called a creative leap in the problem-solving process.

Without being entirely conscious of it, what emerged was an understanding that the big sustainability challenge of today is sustainable decisions. Wherever I looked, there seemed a need for the designer's skill to create safe spaces for groups of people to express themselves (have control and choice), and to make decisions that all are happy enough to support. And in this, I found a new and emerging discipline that for me harboured the excitement and idealism of modernism in today's world.

This budding discipline was so new that, in following my interest, I attended the second-ever Australasian Facilitators Network conference in 1998, an event that I attended for the next ten years. It is now twenty years since buying into that alternative community and fourteen years since leaving to become a participatory development practitioner.

What I now do is to advocate for all to be included in the decisions that affect them and, more specifically, create the spaces for those people to work together, learn from each other as individuals and, as a collective, change and grow.

Whilst this was a personal journey of change and growth, I started to realise that it is equally possible for humanity to go through such a process – not necessarily the same as my journey, but still a process of change and growth.

Two of the big game changers that will have an impact on our current model of reality are digital technology and climate change. The probability is that digital technology will have exactly the same driving force for change as all previous new technologies. Like the wheel, we can use it for an ambulance or a tank. I sometimes wonder if we're doomed to go through the process set out in those novels spanning three generations between 1890 and 1950. All the certainties, all the givens of those occupying the opening chapters are completely upended by the end of the trilogy. We hear a lot about the unprecedented change that we are going through now, but as the futurist I heard on the radio said, the last 60 years is nothing compared to that between 1890 and 1950. Losing sand on the local beach will be the least of many people's worries.

In this book I provide a link between the built environment and the emerging social age. I use it to explain the background to why I think it is not incomprehensible for humanity to be in the process of another period of change and growth, a step into a completely different version of reality to anything we've experienced before.

I then describe some of the theory behind how we can build the necessary spaces for this to occur, and provide examples of both the tools and techniques I use.

There is no shortage of documentation describing the advantages of people collaborating on the decisions that affect them. There is no shortage of programs espousing the need for the community to be engaged in those decisions. What I set out here is why I believe this is not happening enough and, based primarily on my own experiences in the field, what might be done to increase the opportunities for change and growth to occur.

This is not a prescriptive 'The Way To Do It' but rather some techniques and ways of thinking that I'm currently finding quite useful, and which might help in making such a transition more enjoyable.

CHAPTER 1

Setting the stage

Stories can be told in many ways, and cities hold a lot of stories. Individual buildings tell us a lot about the people who built and use them; their culture, their everyday lives, their social organisation, their beliefs, hopes and dreams. As with all media, a characteristic of cities is that they can be an indicator, or language, that can tell stories as well as being the story itself, as Marshall McLuhan described in his book *The medium is the massage*. (The title was a printer's error, the original being *The medium is the message*.) The city and the buildings that contribute to it is both the medium for this story and the message.

For instance, Australian cities were once dotted with family-owned milk bars and small suburban shopping centres. There was a visual similarity to them all that reflected the similar products they sold. They were viable because many people had little access to cars, and the milk bars were within easy walking distance to many houses. Nowadays traditional milk bars are hard to find (Figure 1.1) but there are large supermarkets in abundance – most within a short drive away from housing. Cars have become more affordable, and the spacing of the supermarkets compared with the older milk bars and corner stores reflects this. At the same time the grocery business is no longer the province of the small business person. The difference in size of the supermarkets indicate that food production and distribution has over time become more consolidated and is now the province of different players within society than it once was. The small business retailers and family farmers might have once had power, but now it is the realm of corporate agribusiness and retailers.

Thus, whilst perhaps obvious, what we can learn by looking at the urban environment is the idea of change. Buildings and the urban environment can illustrate how new and different ways of doing things have occurred in the past, and in the process illustrate how the idea that change is part of western or modern culture in its own right. Samuel Johnson might have told his friend Boswell 'when a man is tired of London, he is tired of life' but in 1772 (the time of this quote) there was no effective sewage treatment, no running water and little in the way of medical services. Thankfully London has changed since then (Figure 1.2).

Figure 1.1 The archetypal Aussie corner store. Selling a wide variety of products, there was one within walking distance of almost everyone's house.

Figure 1.2 William Hogarth, *The Rake's Progress*, the *Tavern Scene*. London in the eighteenth century might have been glamorous to Samuel Johnson, but he probably died from lead poisoning – he kept a substantial wine collection in lead-lined vats.

If culture can be described as being 'it is the way we do things around here', then both in real terms and within the mythology of cities, it is the urban environments that best illustrate the idea of change as a cultural attribute. It does not mean, though, that change is unique to cities, because change has been an integral part of the planet since the beginning of time. Neither does it mean that cities as we know them are inevitable. It is just that historically the built environment has been at the centre of social and cultural expression and because change is at the core of our present predicaments (generally, there is either too much of it, whatever it is, or too little) our relationship with the city and built environment is important. It is not so much a cyclical argument as an expression of the interconnectedness that exists between culture and the built environment, the built environment and change. Modern cities are both centres of unsustainable lifestyles, yet

[Not all] cultures have the notion of innovation that is the hallmark of the Western world.[1]

potentially also an indicator of something different emerging.

Looking back at the history of the world, it's possible to see clear differences between, say, the Stone Age and the Iron Age but perhaps with the exception of the extinction of the dinosaurs, it was not a sudden or abrupt change that happened overnight. The transition from one form of 'normal life' to another is not like walking through a door (one minute you are in one reality, the next in another), but something far messier.

In general, cultural stereotypes present great resistance to change and to their own redefinition. Culture, often appears fixed to the observer at any one point in time because cultural mutations occur incrementally. Cultural change is a long-term process.[2]

Thus when we are living in a certain period of time, it is difficult to see how life might be different in the future other than as an extension of the present. Almost all research of the present results in rates of change extrapolated into the future with dire (or amazing) predictions. History books often document change as a series of sequential catalytic events: X happened, and then Y happened, and then Z happened. Whilst there are often such events or 'tipping points' that force accelerated change over a short period of time – a particular battle for instance, or the invention of a new technology such as the internet–in practice change is usually dependent on more than a single event. The forces and dynamics leading up to what is seen to be a catalytic event are usually a complex interwoven web of compounding trajectories. However there are clearly identifiable periods throughout history, such as the Cambrian period, or that of the dinosaurs. It wasn't as if on a given day in 2400 BC everyone woke up thinking 'Today I am going to throw out the old flint, and make a bronze knife'. What actually happened was a long process of decline in the use of stone tools, and the gradual adoption of bronze. It was as if there was a world-wide wave of change.

Waves of change

The idea of 'waves of change' can be expressed diagrammatically as a rolling wave at a set point in time, with decaying practices, accepted norms, emergent concepts and off-the-wall things on the horizon (Figure 1.3). This pattern can be seen in all kinds of disciplines and areas of endeavour, from aeroplane design to methods of voting, from clothing to ways of bringing up children. I'm sure that if you think of your own trade or discipline you could identify its decaying, current and emerging practices. A unique characteristic of the city is that it is possible to see these phenomena historically laid out and recorded at any given time in history.

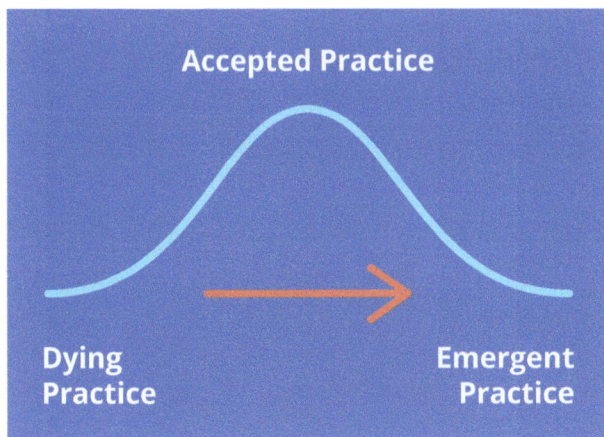

Figure 1.3 At any given time, there can be seen both accepted practice (what we do now), emergent practice (what seem to be new and radical, but we might all be doing soon) and dying practice (what we used to do a lot of, but less nowadays)

Thus one series of 'waves of change' that can be seen in modern cities is the technological drivers for city form. Going back in time to the medieval period, the big drivers of city form were usually protection (in the form of creating city walls) and what could be built from local materials (without power tools), and responding to local geography. Access points in the form of gates in the city walls reflected where people were travelling already. (Figure 1.4) During the fifteenth century, Europeans began to colonise the new worlds and to create new cities. After the initial village settlement, which was generally dictated by

Figure 1.4 St. Swithun's Gate, Winchester. The nature of city form in the middle ages was determined by where people travelled already, the need for physical protection and local materials.

Figure 1.5 In the 1750s, the fastest way to travel long distances was by sailing ship.

access to the sea, the big drivers for how these new cities were laid out and grew continued to be determined by the access to water. Sails and sailing ships were the dominant technology of the day to move people and goods, and for communication (Figure 1.5), Amsterdam and Venice having their beginnings and heydays at this time.

In this period the new cities of the world (such as New York, Sydney, Hobart) grew around the natural water system and sail technology. However by the nineteenth century the driver for city development was the railways, a far more adaptable and flexible transport and communication system than sailing ships. Cities such as Melbourne, Pittsburgh and Delhi were all developed around a rail system (Figure 1.6).

Figure 1.6 Bottom Points Lapstone (little Zig Zag) Rail Road, NSW, 1870.

Just as railways provided a far more flexible system than waterways, the car and freeway became even more adaptable and user-friendly than rail for those that could afford it. The planning and development of new cities that emerged after the year 1900 was primarily determined by where cars and roads were built. New suburbs, new satellite cities, even whole new cities such as Canberra, Houston and Brasilia were determined not by waterways or railways, but by the road system.

As with many other national tram and railway systems, railways in the United Kingdom, once the lifeblood of the nation, were in the 1960s decimated by the Beeching Plan, just as the first of the new motorway system was being constructed.

> ...during the 1960s 'Beeching's Axe' fell on 2,128 stations and more than 67,000 British Rail jobs.[3]

By this time the car, from its early beginnings at the turn of the century, had established itself as the pre-eminent transport system. When the first motorway was constructed in the UK in1959, people cheered from the bridges (Figure 1.7). Enabling road traffic flow is nowadays one of the biggest determinants of city form.

Figure 1.7 The opening of Britain's first long-distance motorway (M1), built to beat the jams, was greeted with great enthusiasm.

Thus in turn each of these waves of changing technologies have made their physical mark on the older cities of the developed world, each in their own way further transforming our cities and influencing our lifestyles (Figure 1.8). As well as these technological systems there are other waves of change that can be seen to have occurred within our cities and buildings. One is the social underpinnings of contemporary society.

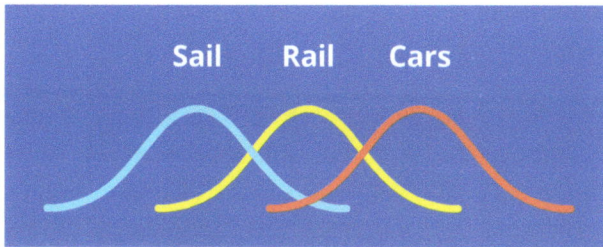

Figure 1.8 The impact of different technologies on city form over time, from the importance of waterways, to railways, to roads has not happened instantaneously, but through waves of change sweeping across the city and its inhabitants.

Those few churches from around 1000 AD that still remain are simple, barn-like affairs with little in the way of ornamentation. Built to accommodate the Christian ceremonies of change and renewal, they probably also acted as something like a community centre to the local farmers (Figure 1.9). To all intents and purposes people at this time would have been living 'at one with nature'. Almost everything would have been achieved against the odds and survival would have been utterly dependent on natural events. Just withstanding each winter without running out of food or freezing to death would have been something to celebrate. I can imagine these small communities of peasants living off the land, with no electricity, no books, long cold winter nights, looking up at the stars and probably terrified about what was going to happen next. They would have heard stories from a variety of people explaining the universe, including those from travelling monks. I suspect that working together to create a communal hall

that celebrated these new ideas of hope would have been very special to those early builders.

As the Christian religion took on greater importance within society across Europe, its buildings developed and grew increasingly large and more ornate.

This growing opulence reflected a proportionate increase in the power of the church itself within contemporary society. I still find it incredible to think how much time and energy everyday people living without gas and electricity, piped water or even an aspirin must have spent working for their church either directly or indirectly to construct such amazing edifices. Over time, people prospered, the churches got bigger and the technology (whilst still stone) more sophisticated (Figure 1.10). By 1250 the Christian church ruled supreme in Europe. Whilst money was a useful tool for buying and selling produce, what was truly valued within medieval European culture was piety and godliness.

The church's greatest power was its control over people's beliefs about life and, especially, death.[4]

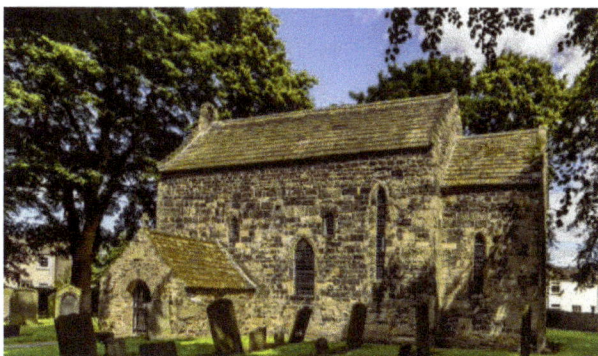

Figure 1.9 Escomb Church. The early character of the building and its resemblance to other early work in Northumberland suggests that it was built in the period 650 to 800.

Figure 1.10 Salisbury Cathedral, the majority of which was constructed between 1220 and 1270.

As well as through the buildings, the all-encompassing nature of this church-based paradigm can be seen in other ways. Margery Kempe (*c.* 1373–after 1438) was the wife of a wealthy businessman. She was possibly illiterate, but able to afford a scribe and recorded her life in what is known as 'the book'.

Although Kempe has sometimes been depicted as an 'oddity' or a 'madwoman', recent scholarship on vernacular theologies and popular practices of piety suggest she was not as odd as she might appear. Her Book is revealed as a carefully constructed spiritual and social commentary.[5]

Whilst the chronicles of Margery Kempe might give the impression to have been written by someone deeply eccentric if not actually delusional, it is more likely that they reflect the real concerns, way of life and worldview so different to ours that there are almost no common reference points. In other words, those alive in 1250 were not 'just like us' without electricity; their whole world, their whole reality, was different to ours.

The middle of the thirteenth century could be referred to as a 'golden age' for the church and its members in Europe.

The Church was perhaps the single most powerful institution in medieval life, its influence reaching almost every aspect of people's lives. Its religious observances gave shape to the calendar; its rituals marked important moments in an individual's life (including baptism, confirmation, marriage, holy orders and the last rites); and its teachings underpinned mainstream beliefs about morality, the meaning of life and the afterlife.[6]

At this time the church in its many forms was at its most powerful and influential. The Crusades were well organised and managed, even if not always successful. The church was at the centre of a huge capital works program that reflected its power as an institution, and its members' power within society. For almost everyone it would have represented the only reality imaginable. Whilst we might struggle to understand their world, they would have no conception of ours at all. Or even of the world just 500 years later in 1750.

Five hundred years later, in 1750, the life and worldview of all classes of people would have been very different. In 1750 there are similar indicators that illustrate the 'golden age' of the landed gentry. One indicator is how country-house building in the UK reached its zenith from the late seventeenth century until the mid-eighteenth century; these houses were often completely built or rebuilt in their entirety by one eminent architect in the most fashionable architectural style of the day. This in itself was something completely new. The churches and cathedrals built in what is now known as 'Gothic' architecture was a way of building with stone or timber to create a space that reflected Christian rites and theology. As much a reflection of a general reaction to the corruption within the church as a desire for a new way to organise the world, the Renaissance architects were inspired by Greek and Roman temples as a style, just as philosophers and thinkers were attracted to those civilisations as ways to organise society.

It was a reflection of a completely new worldview compared to that which existed in 1250. Young men on the grand tour, looking at not just ruins but also the architecture of Piranesi and the work of Michelangelo, would have been exposed to new ideas of urban and civic thought. Through colonialism the world of the gentry was being exported right across the globe. But it also brought back different ideas, such as concepts of urban design that included parks and boulevards. During the medieval period this would have been unheard of; study at that time was limited to the Bible, stories of the saints and discussions on morality and piety.

Thus most often deriving their cues from Greek and Roman temples, these eighteenth-century palaces reflect a whole new way of looking at the world, albeit romantically. The word 'renaissance' referred to what was perceived at the time as the renaissance of traditional empires and philosophies, rudely interrupted by the church and the middle ages. Networking and people's status in society were paramount (Figure 1.11). The palaces would often have a suite of Baroque state apartments – typically in enfilade – reserved for the most eminent guests, the entertainment of whom was of greatest importance to maintaining and gaining the required power of the owner (Figure 1.12).

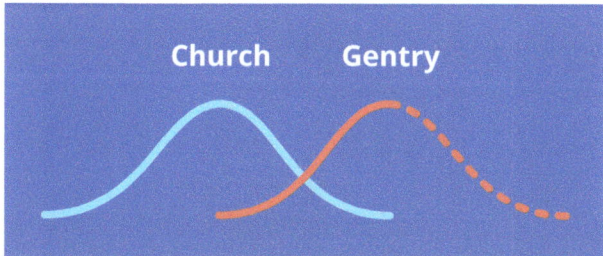

Figure 1.11 Whilst the church was all powerful in 1250 Europe, it was the landed gentry that ruled supreme in 1750. The grand buildings being constructed in this time were no longer churches, but secular palaces.

Figure1.12 Blenheim Palace. Designed by Vanbrugh in 1705, it is considered one of the finest of the emerging non-ecclesiastical buildings of the time.

By 1750 the whole of society was organised in a strictly hierarchical manner, with everyone aware of their station in life, and with few exceptions the hierarchy was accepted by all parties. For those with power, any consideration of others was limited to how well treated the lower classes were. When relating to those of higher status, the concern was how well you served. As a class of people, the landed gentry exuded confidence and the rightness of their version of civilised man in the world. No longer

pious stained-glass portraits of saints, the images that hung on the walls of those that could afford it were pictures of themselves and their property. Their greatest concern was probably their status in society. Whilst imperfect in many ways, the capacity for people to own and control land provided the basis for an amazing explosion of culture and productivity (Figure 1.13).

Figure 1.13 Bank Hall, 1750 (currently Warrington Town Hall). Designed by James Gibbs for the Patten family, wealthy merchants. Whilst not nobility, the family gained status in owning land. This is reflected in the style and size of house they inhabited.

Whilst this new reality provided considerably more freedoms and possibilities compared to the strictures of the church, this worldview also proved to be temporary with its own built-in self-destruction. In this instance the self-destruct implant was in the overarching adherence of the hierarchical class system, combined with the need for people with problem-solving capacities to support the development of both trade and military conquest. This led to a further wave of change.

By the1950s, there was a new world order (Figure 1.14). This period was probably the 'golden age' for what might be called the technical professional sector of society. For all of Marx's theories about the inevitability of class warfare and the overthrow of the capitalist system, he failed to see the rise of this new reality. However he would not have been alone

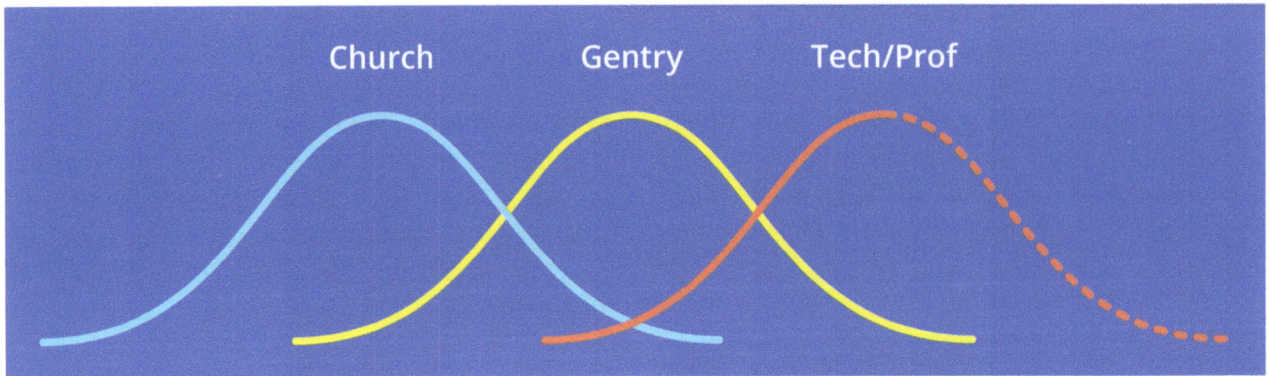

Figure 1.14 The new world order in 1950 belonged to the technical professional.

in failing to foresee the possibility of this emerging technically educated class and its impact on the world. The idea of 'society' as 'the natural order' of things being eroded and overtaken by those who could think quickly and solve complicated technical problems would have been too far outside the box (Figure 1.15).

Just as most people living in 1250 could probably conceive of no other reality than a theocracy, it is almost certain that neither could most in 1750 imagine a world not built on rigid social class lines. Thus during the period from their emergence as a power in their own right during the 1800s, this segment of society achieved a point from about 1950 to 1965 when they could do no wrong. In this period they could spray whole suburbs with DDT without informing anybody. They could develop and release new drugs with little or no scrutiny (thalidomide), invent and promote new building materials (asbestos cement), construct new freeways, airports and dams with little or no dissension, and if there was disagreement it certainly gained little traction.

In the 1950s and 1960s, this segment of society were effectively omnipotent. The idea of a technically sophisticated civilisation was represented in the widespread adoption of a design philosophy that clearly and unambiguously reflected this new reality. Clean lines, no decoration, exhortations for form to follow function, these buildings reflected desirable business and technical efficiencies and values (Figure 1.16).

Figure 1.15 Isambard Kingdom Brunel in front of the chains of the Great Eastern, 1857. The gentry might have owned the land, but their Empire was increasingly dependent on the knowledge and expertise held by the technical professionals.

The [Seagram] building's crisp, clean lines epitomize the standardization and impersonality that became synonymous with the modern corporation.' [7]

With few exceptions (some of the landed gentry were still fighting a rearguard action), it was generally held that only good could be done by those with the fortune to be technically and professionally trained in our society at this time. My parents might have told me 'We don't mind what you do, dear, as long as you're happy' but the subtext was 'doctor, lawyer, teacher, engineer'.

A curious but consistent paradox is that often the most resolved, most expressive articulations of the essence of a particular wave have occurred after the 'golden age' of that period (Figure 1.17). The US Capitol building is one of the most accomplished examples of neo-classicism. King's College chapel completed (eventually) in 1544 is one of the greatest expressions of Gothic architecture, This beautiful, graceful space is all created from load-bearing stonework – no CAD, no steel, no concrete, just one stone on top of another. Buildings such as the Gherkin and the Shard in London demonstrate high levels of technical sophistication to achieve a seemingly simple design expression. There can be no doubt that many people have benefited from the opportunities and achievements of the technical/scientific class. And, as with all previous waves, those that have benefited most are the least desirous of change, improved

Figure 1.16 Seagram building, designed by Mies van Der Rohe, completed 1960

King's College Chapel. Completed in 1544, perhaps the ultimate gothic building.

The United States Capitol, commenced in 1793. The purpose of the building might have been revolutionary (breaking away from the British) but the architectural expression is entirely that of stately homes such as Blenheim Palace.

The Gherkin, a striking example of corporate power and technical expertise.

Figure 1.17 It is usually after the peak of acceptance of a particular way of doing things that the most expressive architectural examples of the period are created.

lifestyle and the potential of individual recognition of worth being two of the great benefits of the advance of the technical professionals.

When Khruschev told Nixon, 'Whether you like it or not, history is on our side. We will bury you',[8] the area of disagreement was about what might be the superior ideology regarding social organisation. At this time of the Cold War, nobody disputed the rightness of a future underpinned by the technical professionals. In a similar political context, Harold Wilson in 1963 said that Britain 'will be forged in the white heat of the [technological] revolution'.

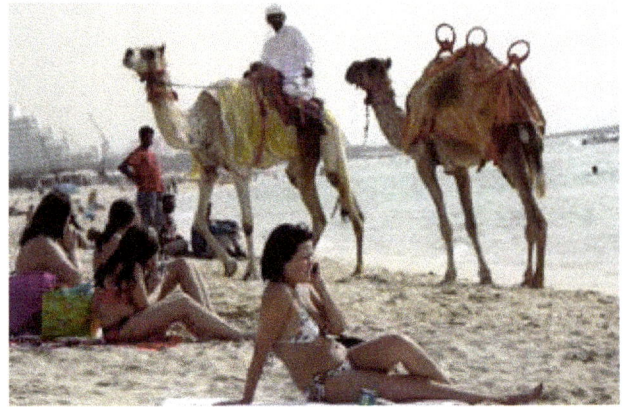

Figure 1.18 Expats on the beach in Dubai. These are not the ones working on the construction sites or as maids and nannies.

The actual words spoken by Wilson in a speech on 1 October 1963 to the Labour Party Conference were: 'We are redefining and we are restating our socialism in terms of the scientific revolution.... The Britain that is going to be forged in the white heat of this revolution will be no place for restrictive practices or outdated methods on either side of industry.' Wilson succeeded in associating his government with technological innovation, in contrast to the perceived old-fashioned ideas in the Conservative Party.[9]

Indicators of this sector's continuing status as the dominant sector in society can be found in how our current conception of the city generally suits this sector of society very well. Excepting those that have become rich and powerful through inheritance or luck, the primary (legal) beneficiaries of contemporary cities are those who have the greatest capacity to undertake Abstract Rational Thought (ART). Those who have the capacity to carry out complicated tasks such as designing or constructing rapid transport systems, high-rise buildings, complicated pieces of policy and intricate financial products by and large find the contemporary city not a bad place to be (Figure 1.18).

They have the better paying jobs in government and private sector organisations, together with access to the education system that ensures that their children will also benefit from becoming one of the same class.

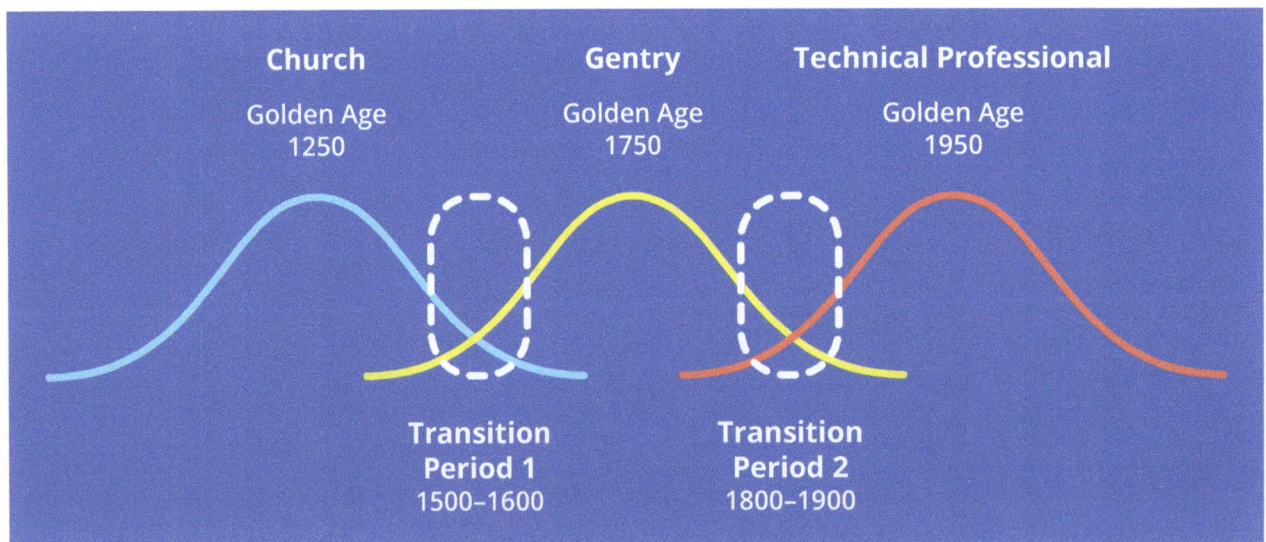

Church	Gentry	Technical Professional
Golden Age 1250	Golden Age 1750	Golden Age 1950

Transition Period 1
1500–1600

Transition Period 2
1800–1900

Figure 1.19 Transition periods: what happens between the Golden Ages

14

Transition periods

After, and even during, any 'golden age' ideas emerge that, whilst seemingly inconsequential, collectively challenge the established orthodoxy. In any series of waves, there is a transition period between each wave (Figure 1.19). Transition periods are messy. They are often times of anachronisms and false starts, yet also of wonderful creativity. A transition period displays elements of both the emergence of the new and decay in the old paradigm. Thus between each of these major waves of social organisation there are multiple indicators of something new emerging.

After 1250 the church continued to hold substantial power and influence within society, but an increasing number of setbacks to its authority and culture occurred. By no means all challenges to the status quo were political, or even the result of new ways of thinking. A very particular setback to established society of the Middle Ages were the plague events of 1450 and 1660. These events decimated the European population and at the time were inexplicable, and thus acts of God – a vengeful god that was not happy with current society.

In the same period the church as an institution was shaken when the English king (Henry VIII, 1491–1547) expressed dissent with the Pope's ruling concerning Henry's desired divorce. This indeed might have been a major tipping point, for the eruption associated with the break-up of the Christian church at this time left few untouched.

[Copernicus'] epochal book, De revolutionibus orbium coelestium (On the Revolutions of the Celestial Spheres), published in 1543 just before he died, is often regarded as the starting point of modern astronomy and the defining epiphany that began the Scientific Revolution.[10]

Additionally, during this period new technologies were being developed, such as the printing press and better agricultural techniques. The

Over the centuries, the English Parliament progressively limited the power of the English monarchy, which arguably culminated in the English Civil War and the trial and execution of Charles I in 1649. After the restoration of the monarchy under Charles II, and the subsequent Glorious Revolution of 1688, the supremacy of parliament was a settled principle and all future English and later British sovereigns were restricted to the role of constitutional monarchs with limited executive authority.[11]

printing press, initially developed to publish the Bible, quickly became used to spread all kinds of radical ideas concerning its interpretation. Improved agricultural techniques provided more food, but were far more suited to individual control of land than common use and thus in turn undermined the then traditional way of doing things.

The characteristics of this transition period can be seen in buildings of the period. During the Middle Ages, domestic houses were either fortresses or farmhouses. Gradually a new architectural expression emerged that used the architectural and construction elements of the church, but for a new purpose.

Figure 1.20 Cotehele in Cornwall was not so much designed as constructed as a large farm house. The main phases of building appear to have been between 1485–89 and 1489–1520.

In essence, Cotehele House in Cornwall is just a large medieval farmhouse (Figure 1.20). But its large windows and doors could only have been built after years of practice building churches, knowledge that was gradually incorporated and adapted into the art and architecture of the emerging landed gentry. Hampton Court (Figure 1.21) was commissioned by Cardinal Wolsey, Henry VIII's chief advisor at the time in 1514, who wanted a home away from the intrigues

Figure 1.21 Hampton Court Palace, begun in 1514. Commissioned by Cardinal Wolsey, Henry VIII later commandeered it. Architecturally it is a mixture of gothic cathedral and fortress elements, though the function is residential.

Figure1.22 Hardwick Hall, more glass than wall. Designed and built in 1590-97.

and hassles of the court in London. The front entrance looks very much like a castle (except they are not real fortifications) with large windows and a symmetrical elevation. A short time later Robert Smythson (sometimes referred to as England's first architect) was designing numerous houses for the emerging new elite (Figure 1.22). As well as large windows Hardwick Hall has a verandah on the front, and balustrades at the top of the walls hiding the roof. Far from being a fortress or Gothic church, it is more a reflection of the growing interest in ancient Greek and Roman civilisations.

There are other ways in which this messy transition period is expressed by remnants of the old order mixed in with the emerging new order. An example is how the paintings of the Renaissance are often based on scenes from the Bible, but also include portraits of the patron in the crowd. Something akin to taking a selfie at a major event: 'Look, I was there!'

Thus some of the characteristics of a transition period would include:

- new ideas that challenge the orthodoxy of the status quo

- new and emergent building types

- new technologies

- emergent ideas about social organisation

- expressions of unsuccessful attempts to maintain the existing order or decaying practice

- expressions of nostalgia for the 'good old days' of previous ages

- expressions of disquiet with the current order

- within the built environment, strange hybrids that combine elements of the new with the old.

In the period from 1800 to 1900 there are examples of these changes, just as there were in the earlier period of change between the unquestioned power of the church and the rise of the landed gentry.

In the second period of fundamental change, there are clear examples of strange hybrids within the built environment. An example of a nostalgic expression of bygone days is the new Palace of Westminster (UK Houses of Parliament) (Figure 1.23) designed in the Gothic style by Sir Charles Barry in 1835. It was quite consciously determined that the architectural expression should be 'English' based on either an Elizabethan or Gothic vocabulary.

Figure 1.23 UK Houses of Parliament. During the 1800s there emerged a serious 'style war' between those that favoured the 'Classical' or the 'Gothic', based on arguments of morality and purity.

A similar nostalgic approach was found in the Arts and Crafts movement, which had its heyday in the late 1800s. Houses were designed to look

Figure 1.24 Philip Webb, Red House, Bexley Heath, 1859. Note how this is designed to look more like the Cothele manor, not a Greek temple.

like traditional farmhouses and cottages (Figure 1.24), and novelty buildings such as the Brighton Pavilion appeared. During this period there were many passionate arguments about the true or correct architectural styles, often linked to notions of morality and purity attributed to the earlier medieval period.

With the rise in the corporation, new buildings such as post offices and banks also became necessary, which for want of any better idea often used the same architectural expression as the stately homes of the gentry (Figure 1.25). It was only in the 1920s that the idea of having an architecture that consciously reflected and articulated concepts of science and technology emerged.

Figure 1.25 One of the first purpose-built post offices, St. Martins in the Grand, looking like a stately home, but in fact a corporate office.

Over the last forty years there have been all kinds of hybrids, contradictions and other indicators of change. The overt romanticism of postmodernism continues in a debased form in every developer's lexicon, and similarly there is an active 'back to nature' movement. Within the science and technology domain computers have enabled buildings to become ever more sophisticated in both the spaces and forms created, as well as in the construction systems employed to build them. However, none of this can truly reflect a serious response to our current reality: the reality of ever more unpredictable climatic conditions combined with the many indicators of failure in the traditional approaches to present-day social problems.

Architecturally this can even be seen in the advent of instant cities such as that created by the Occupy movement, and a complete failure of meeting the right to shelter of the growing numbers of homeless in an affluent country such as Australia (Figure 1.26). Around the world, there are more people living in what are sometimes referred to as informal settlements than ever before. These are communities characterised by insufficient access to resources, services and security of tenure (Figure 1.27).

Homelessness in Australia has increased 13.7% in 5 years

- ABS Census, 2016

116,427 Australians now have no home

Figure 1.26 Effectively defining the new non-architecture of the poor in the developed world, there is not even the possibility of creating an informal settlement.

Figure 1.27. Durban, South Africa. An outcome of people creating a city with minimal, if any, official support and restricted access to resources.

These communities are all pointing to the need of something completely different emerging.

One of the few consistent characteristics of change is the nature of birth, flowering and gradual decline. What happens on the journey is the interesting part.

The argument for change to current mainstream city life exists at many levels, and most compelling is the idea of environmental sustainability. All the indicators are that contemporary modern cities are completely unsustainable. There is no doubt that to live in an environment that comes anywhere near to being sustainable means doing things very differently. History suggests that what we experience as being the only reality is not necessarily so. In fact, there are many people today talking about change, though not necessarily with the same idea in mind.

But if it's not 'more of the same, but better', what might it be? After all, technology has provided lots in the past, and innovation is a core precept of current society. And nobody, least of all I, want a return to the bad old days.

Donald Trump, Pauline Hanson, and others on the 'alt right' (Figure 1.28) might not express a very sophisticated view of the world, but what they do is to articulate and give voice to the

Let's take back control

Leave

Figure 1.28 Brexit. A situation where self-serving opportunists use the poor's disempowerment by the technical professional segment to foster their own interests.

many that feel disenchanted and disenfranchised in their everyday life.

Throughout history there have been soothsayers and prophets varying from apocalyptic to utopian to gee whiz. The common thread is that every prophesy is constructed according to the physical and cultural conditions of the individual within society making those predictions. Predictions are thus usually extrapolations of activities occurring in the present, projected into the future by a multiplier of some form.

Thus predictions range from the biblical to the fashion editor, and also predictions for the personal and the general. Which ones to believe? Which will prove to be true? The end of the world on 1 January 2000? Or as it was not then....when? Or perhaps, viewing through a different lens, bio-engineering will be the saviour of the planet? There is just no shortage of predictions. (The scientist, environmentalist and futurist James Lovelock, inventor of the Gaia concept, believes that there is every possibility that the human species will be reduced to a few breeding pairs at the poles.) But to date there is no accurate and reliable basis on which to determine which will come true.

The Gaia hypothesis also known as the Gaia theory or the Gaia principle, proposes that living organisms interact with their inorganic surroundings on Earth to form a synergistic and self-regulating, complex system that helps to maintain and perpetuate the conditions for life on the planet.[12]

Prediction and design

Prediction is one way of thinking about the future; another is to work towards creating a future that we want. This is design, and what lies at the core of those phrases 'evidence-based practice' and 'research-led decision making'.

The essential difference between designing the future and predicting the future is one of action.

Predicting the future is looking at what is happening now, and guessing what might happen in the future. Design is a process of envisaging a desired future, and working to achieve it, whilst at the same time being aware of the current situation or reality. Four essential components of design are:

1. An articulated desired vision, or imagined desirable end state.

2. An understanding of what is currently happening pertaining to the topic of the vision.

3. A sequence of steps or process to get from the present state to the desired future.

4. An understanding of the resources at hand to create action.

Of these, setting the vision is a critical component.

The components of a good vision statement. They should be a means by which we describe a desired outcome that invokes a vivid mental picture of our goal.[13]

Setting the vision

A letter writer to the *Guardian Weekly* (March 2010) expressed a vision for the future that many of its readers (educated, technically proficient, inquisitive) would probably be happy enough to adopt: 'There's general agreement on the destination: a planet where all sentient beings can grow, work, play, create, eat, shit and sleep in perpetuity and safety'. The writer then stated that the big problem is that we don't know how to get there. As we live in an age where if you fail to plan, you plan to fail, this is not a good situation. However it does set up the challenge, and a challenge that is open to a wide spectrum of discourse. As Enrique Penalosa, former mayor of Bogata, Colombia, stated: 'We know a lot about the ideal environment for a happy whale or a happy mountain gorilla. We're far less clear about what constitutes an ideal environment for a happy human being.'[14]

The challenge is how do we go about achieving the vision? Perhaps what is emerging is something that is more inclusive, more diverse, something that does not just rely on those that are quick thinkers from the right school to be the only ones with the power to effect change.

CHAPTER 2

The emerging development paradigm

There is much to celebrate about our modern world. As well as improved life expectancies and qualities of life, we have developed a culture of change that places value on innovation, risk-taking and seeking improvement on what is the current norm. There are many advances in understanding the uncertainties that exist in the field of quantum physics, and huge advances in mapping the universe in which we exist. There has also been much work studying both ourselves as people and the planet we live on. A key piece of contemporary scientific observation is the idea of complexity.

Complexity

When I work with groups of people in the area of innovation and change, I often start with a simple questioning sequence. The first is to ask, what were Copernicus & Galileo famous for? The answers are often a bit vague, but someone will usually remember something about the earth going around the sun. I then ask what happened to Galileo and again someone will come up with an answer along the lines that he was imprisoned. Again, when I ask why, there is a general recognition that his observation challenged the ruling belief system and power of the church. Then I enquire whether they know what Newton was famous for. Again there is some vague memory about apples and gravity. Then I ask if Newton invented gravity. To this there is a resounding no. We then have a brief discussion about the importance of these observations at their time in the evolution of people on the planet. My third question is to ask what Rittel and Webber are famous for. They usually have no idea. The answer is that Rittel and Webber (amongst others) noticed and documented in 1973 the idea of complicated and complex systems.

Their paper, 'Dilemmas in a General Theory of Planning', describes how there are both complicated and complex systems in which the nature of the problems that reside in them are correspondingly Tame and Wicked. An example of a complicated system is the wiring on an aeroplane (Figure 2.1), a highly sophisticated system, but one in which it is possible to determine which switch will make which light work. If given enough time and resources, the answer is achievable and demonstrable (either the light works or it doesn't), and the problem can be termed Tame. This is in contrast to the complex system in which the passengers on the aeroplane exist. There is no one way in which to resolve a problem that might exist between the football team, the little old lady and the jet-lagged flight attendant. Not only are there multiple definitions of the problem, there are also infinite solutions that in their own way exist on a scale of rightness as to solution. It is this infinitely variable condition of problem and solution that is characteristic of a Wicked problem that exists within a complex system.

Flying to the moon was a great achievement, incredibly complicated, with many different

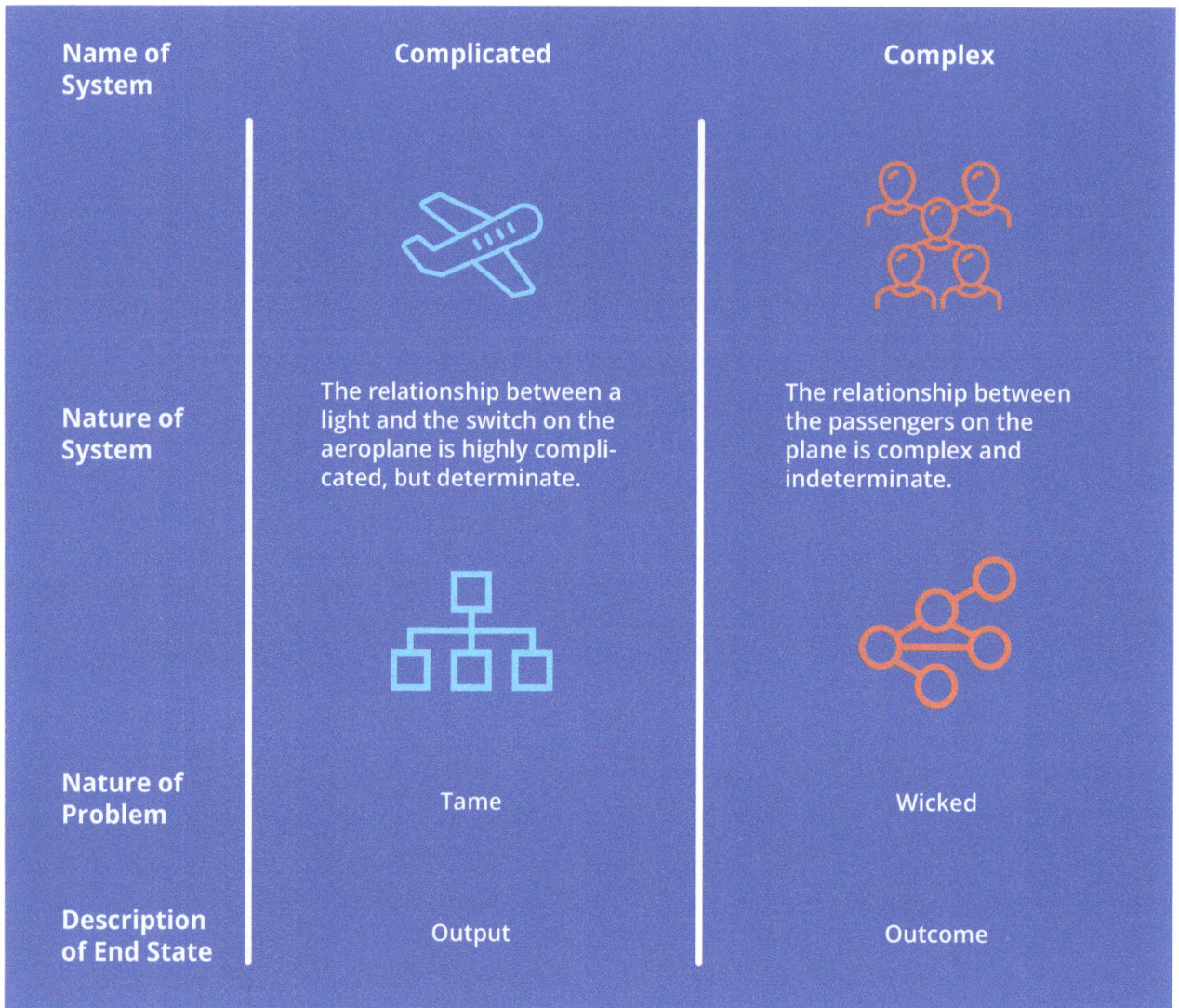

Name of System	Complicated	Complex
Nature of System	The relationship between a light and the switch on the aeroplane is highly complicated, but determinate.	The relationship between the passengers on the plane is complex and indeterminate.
Nature of Problem	Tame	Wicked
Description of End State	Output	Outcome

Figure 2.1 An interpretation by the author of the work by Rittel and Webber.

design parameters, but it was a Tame problem. Neil Armstrong and colleagues either got there and back, or didn't. Luckily for them, they did.

Whilst Rittel and Webber talked of Tame and Wicked problems, more commonly used words to describe the differences within the systems have emerged, in particular words such as Outputs and Outcomes. It can be problematic that sometimes the same words are used to describe both conditions, but I like the word Outputs to describe those concrete tangible, measurable things that exist at a point in time, and the word Outcome to describe the effect within the system. Just for fun, try the quiz 'Which is an output, which an outcome?' (Figure 2.2).

	Output	Outcome
A report		
Angry neighbours		
Festival		
Shopping Centre		
Productive workforce		
Warm inner glow		
Healthy river		
A plan		
Policy Document		
Resilient community		

Fig 2.2 Quiz: Tick which is an output, and which an outcome?

Complex
Emergent Practice
Probe-Sense-Respond

The "market" philosophy provides a mechanism that reflects complexity. It is an enrepreneurial approach to the world. There is no one solution—housing is a verb. **People express themselves differently.**

Complicated
Good Practice
Sense-Act-Respond

Most government policy approaches view issues as a complicated problem e.g., develop a prototype, and replicate it across the nation. **Provide lots of people with a house.**

Chaotic
Novel Practice
Act-Sense-Respond

As weather and social systems become more erratic, there will be an increasing need for flexibility. **We've build the camps, but what next?**

Simple
Best Practice
Sense-Categorise-Respond

A simple system sees all problems as simple e.g., a homeless person needs a house. **Traditional societies developed single type solutions to housing.**

Figure 2.3 The Cynefin Model by Dave Snowden. Architectural examples provided by author.

No doubt you found some of them harder to answer than others, and you'd like to check the answers at the back of the book. Unfortunately there are none there and instead I request that you ask your friends what they think. If you ask a number of people, you will probably find that there is consensus on the extremes, but that there is some discussion on some of the others. This is just one of the characteristics of what we are working with: there is often agreement on the extremes, but differences of opinion and interpretation in the middle.

Another theorist exploring the differences in the type of problem and the system in which they exist is Dave Snowden, the inventor of the Cynefin framework. This is a conceptual model to describe the nature of problems and the system in which they reside. His description of the difference between a complicated system and a complex system is that you can take a Ferrari to pieces and put it back together, but you can't take a rainforest to pieces and put it back together.

If I interpret the Cynefin framework through an architectural lens (Figure 2.3), I can see that traditional cultures saw housing as a simple problem. We've always built houses like this in our culture. Today, our professional/technical society views the problem of housing as how to build many houses. It has become a complicated, technical problem demanding mass production and efficiencies of scale. The mass-produced solution to housing is similar in all authoritarian regimes, from company housing to communist dictatorships.

An approach to housing that responds to complexity treats housing as a verb. It is something that people do, rather than being a product. It is an outcome of diversity and multiple values. The houses of Drop City built in 1968 by the Merry Pranksters were inspired by Buckminster Fuller, a need to use cheap materials, and various anti-establishment ideals. Whilst this is extreme, the suburban house and its environs is remarkably flexible

and illustrates a wide variety of values and worldviews.

This is different again to the kind of housing people want and need in chaotic situations such as after a natural disaster. Thus on the right-hand side of the model is the currently accepted, mainstream view of the world whilst on the left is a potentially more useful, emergent view of the world.

A third commentator on this new view of the world I have found useful is architect and mathematician Christopher Alexander. In his 1968 article 'The city is not a tree', he explored how whilst it is possible to design a building, it is not possible to design a city. Whilst there are connections (which he called a semi-lattice) between buildings and the city in which they reside, ultimately a city is a reflection of a complex system, not something that can be imagined and constructed in the same way as a single building such as the Sydney Opera House. Thus to take on the problem of creating 'a world in which all sentient beings...etc.', it is necessary to appreciate that the nature of the problem is different to that of creating a new Opera House, or flying to the moon. The Opera House is an Output, our vision of a world for 'all sentient beings...etc.' is an Outcome.

Innovation and change

It might be a different kind of problem, but a singular characteristic of the age of the professional/technical has been the rise in this concept of design. It is design that underpins everything from Stevenson's innovative steam trains in 1830 to the moon landing. The idea of design is more complex than skill, flair or pluck, but still essential to the creation of the products and services of the industrial age.

Google the question, what is design? The answers are many and varied. Some examples are:

- Design is a work process which has a user perspective and drives development based on your specific customer's needs. (www.svid.se/en/What-is-design/)

- Design is the process of imagining and planning the creation of objects, systems, buildings, vehicles, etc. It is about creating solutions for people. (https://www.strate.education/gallery/news/design-definition)

- Design is the creation of a plan or convention for the construction of an object, system or measurable human interaction (as in architectural blueprints, engineering drawings, business processes, circuit diagrams, and sewing patterns). (https://en.wikipedia.org/wiki/Design)

Action Research and Design

Design is often used as a noun, but it is the verb that is important. A designer in any field works through an iterative process towards seeking an ideal solution for each problem, and in the process becomes a more competent designer. Students of any design discipline want more time for design whilst those competent can make it look effortless. Whilst there is always a gap between the image and the reality, you need to start with an idea of what you are designing to achieve. The Sydney Opera House didn't just appear as a finished design, it started as a description of an idea (Figure 2.4), which can be called the vision, followed by considerable

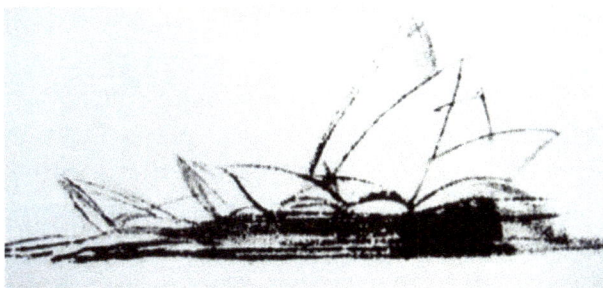

Figure 2.4 An early sketch by Jørn Utzon for the Sydney Opera House design.

work with many challenges to overcome between the initial image and the final reality.

Whatever the product or service desired, it is this process of iterative development that has resulted in change, and in that change new learning and development has occurred. Thus this process of iterative development is a fundamental underpinning to modernity. This process often referred to as design is in my experience the same as Action Learning or Action Research (Figure 2.5). Traditionally it was thought that reading and listening to lectures by the master was a key learning methodology. More recent research suggests that in today's complex world there is no one right way to do anything, and that learning to learn is key. Thus contemporary educational thought asserts that for most people 70 per cent of learning is on the job, 20 per cent through designed experiential learning workshops, and 10 per cent through traditional lectures and book reading.

The Action Learning or design process is effectively the same; it is the function or aim that is different. The designer's main interest is the product at the end, and the educationalist's main interest is the learning that has occurred during the process. What is becoming evident is that those involved in designing and creating products and services also learn. They learn about both their field of endeavour, and about themselves as people. Equally, those involved in Action Research or Action Learning have to create a product of some kind.

Like the Opera House, the moon landing was challenging, difficult work on the edge of many people's technical competence. Neither was a procedural problem requiring the application of best practice. There was no pattern to follow. Working on the project probably also resulted in the individuals in the various teams making some of the best friends of their lives. And even if good friends were not made, the skills to work constructively with people who might have had different ideas to them, but united in seeking a common, clearly defined, tangible problem, were

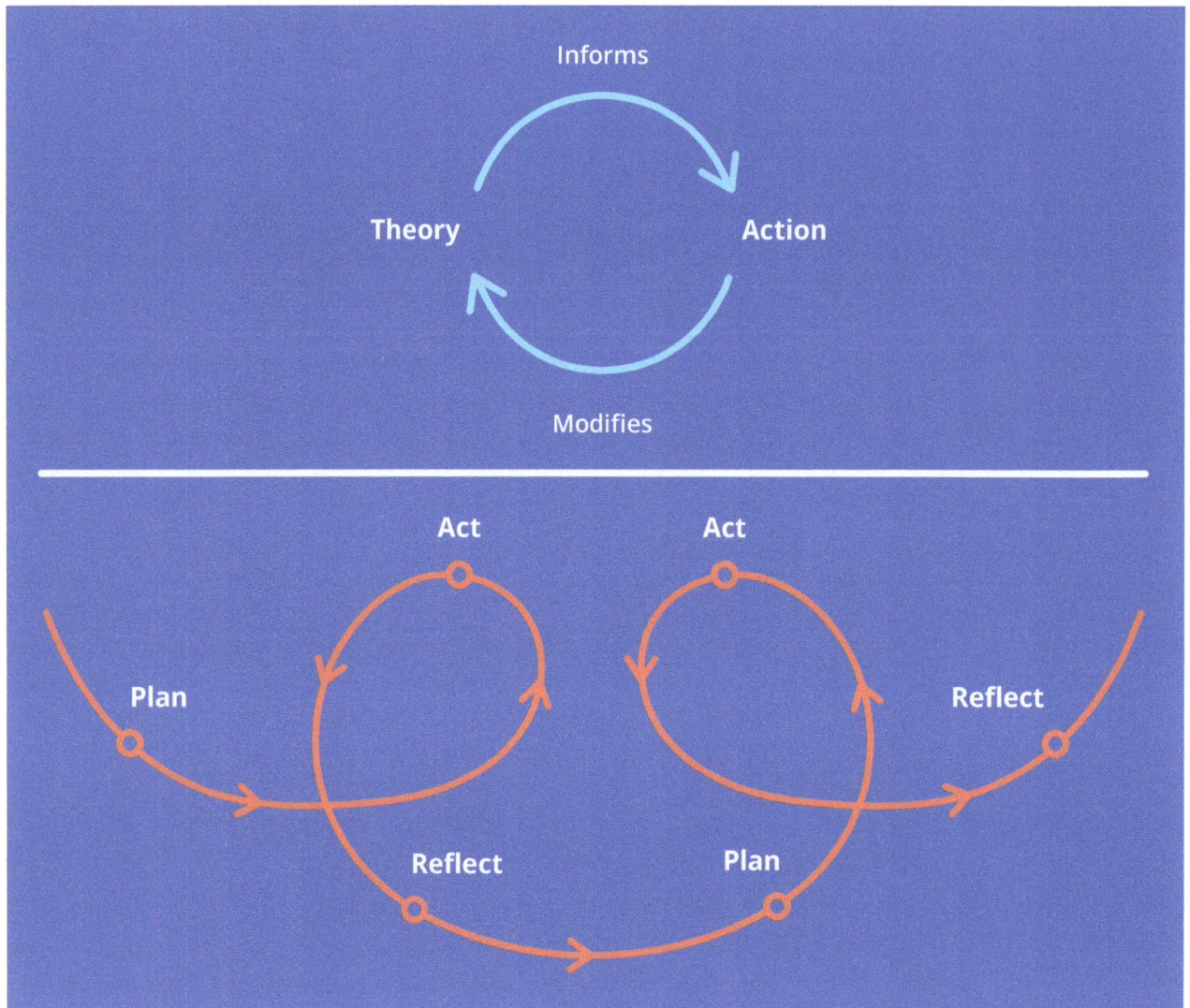

Figure 2.5. The Action Learning model, which has considerable similarities to the design process.

developed. The group was not together to have a good time, or develop bonds with others of different cultural backgrounds, but to solve the real, tangible problem of putting someone on the moon. In the process the individuals developed and grew in both their technical capacities as well as challenged and stretched their personal and interpersonal capacities. For those involved, it was a process of Action Learning.

The learning occurred through being part of the team solving the problem. This is one of the great conceptual changes or leaps that separates the emerging social age and that of the age of the technical/professional. It is the emergence of an understanding that it is through being part

of solving the problem that people learn, develop and grow – by doing what the professional/technicals have done.

Whilst the design process is attributable to the creation of unique outputs, complex systems need a different tool to understand them than the traditional analytical tools useful to understand a complicated system. A common tool or technique used by those interested in working in complex situations is story. Stories can express nuance, lived experience, analogies, parables and many layers of meaning. It is through story that we can make sense of our own world and convey meaning about seemingly random events.

Story 1

When studying architecture, one of my tutors was passionately interested in medieval church architecture, and in particular Chartres Cathedral. At the time I found it really interesting and useful to explore how the medieval masons used geometry and mathematical ratios together with numerology to provide meaning to their decisions. Richness, interest and beauty was achieved in their creations through the multiple layers of connotation underlying every decision. It was this depth of meaning that separated the medieval Gothic churches from the later Victorian churches designed and constructed in a Gothic style. What I learned was that a considered design has to answer at many levels, both-and, and-this, together-with... For example, meets the functional brief **and** keeps the weather out **and** looks good **and** is within budget **and** provides users an appropriate emotional response.

Story 2

As a government architect working in Swaziland I built a number of police stations in the country. Being particularly interested in environmentally sustainable development I would try to use low-tech building materials, passive solar principles and local construction techniques. It was very much a personal quest to create appropriate designs. At this time I also wrote a study about developing a police capital works program in the areas targeted by a World Bank urban upgrading program. In this work I developed a number of options, but in particular I realised that a sustainable decision would require incorporating the views of the many stakeholders in such a program – the police, the ministry of finance, the surrounding communities and numerous others. The realisation was the easy part and I'd like to say that this was some kind of eureka moment that I had, but it's been far more a matter of micro leaps that have resulted in a gradual unfolding of understanding. Something like Barack Obama's evolving acceptance of gay marriage. It was not a sudden moment of understanding. In his own words, he went through a process in which his understanding evolved.

In my experience this gradual change in understanding is more the nature of change and growth than the sudden eureka moment. Even if there are minor sudden flashes of insight along the way these are usually the result of a sustained thinking and problem-solving process.

The creative leap is a mental creative moment in which one discovers and illustrates a new design idea, or restructures and develops an old one...The results from this study show that the creative leap is a sudden mental insight that comes as a result of structuring the design knowledge cycle.[1]

Story 3

It was later, when living on a community title property in northern New South Wales that I really started to understand the depth of challenge that the phrase 'engaging all the stakeholders' really means. At a technical level, the relatively simple governance structure was laid out in a legal document. The property owners would elect a management committee through an annual general meeting. The management committee would then identify development projects and programs and set a levy to finance them. In practice it was unworkable. Those that had bought into the property were attracted because it provided a sense of community, and they presumed that they would be involved in the development of projects and programs. We had the common goal of developing 13 hectares of land, but the real challenges existed in a signiificant one of three development zones. These are the I zone, the We zone, and the It zone.

The I Zone relates to personal development, how it is that over time we as an individual generally become more aware of things, understand things that we didn't understand before, make improvements in our skills and capabilities. As individuals, we were varied in our capacities, but generally most were interested in some kind of individual pursuits leading to growth and change.

The It zone is the area of outputs, that is goods and services: the numbers of trees planted, parties held, weeds removed. Generally, this was not a problem area for us. Most knew enough about passive solar ideas, the advantages of insulation and so on, and were able to build houses that suited needs.

The We zone is our capacity to interact with others. Our capacity to understand and accept another's viewpoint, how we cope when confronted by those that challenge our own conceptions of normal. This was the area of greatest challenge. Achieving agreed decisions was almost impossible within the defined governance structure.

The I and We zones exist within the realm of complexity, the It zone within the realm of complicated. An approximation of what these might look like is Figure 2.6, in which the nodes are the personal capabilities of individuals, the linkages being their capacity to work with others.

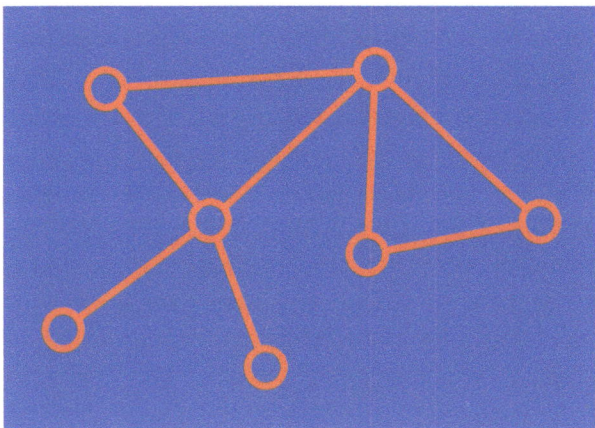

Figure 2.6 A basic illustration of a system made of nodes and linkages.

Inclusion

Whilst I found that there are significant problems associated with people collectively making decisions, I also found many indicators that illustrate both the advantages to people working together to make concrete decisions, and the increasing desire by many to be included in the decisions that affect them, or in which they have an interest.

These indicators are as varied as the rise in the green movement (with battles like stopping the Franklin Dam), the anti-Iraq marches (which was not listened to) and more recently government departments such as the Victorian Department of Environment, Land, Water and Planning publishing a community charter. This document sets out how it will engage with the broader community, with a statement commencing with 'We will work with you to [create] inclusive, sustainable communities'.

Experiments at the industrial level were carried out in as early as the 1950's by such people as the industrial psychologist Fred Emery at the Tavistock Institute. The Institute looked at organisations, and how they might work better, more efficiently and effectively. Their experiments demonstrated the value of self-organised teams within the National Coal Board. In a similar vein, the owner of a large Dutch engineering company adopted and transformed the sociocracy movement from its nineteenth-century Quaker origins into the organisational structure in their factories. Today, it is almost mainstream for organisations to promote the benefits of partnerships with others, consulting stakeholders and innovating with co-design processes. Nowadays there are many contemporary progressive organisations that place considerable emphasis on how employees should relate to each other to be more effective and efficient to achieve desired goals. It is no longer sufficient to be a brilliant academic, or outstanding engineer. You also have to know how to relate to others within the organisation and beyond. The result of these endeavours resides in the realm of complexity; happier people, more innovation, greater customer satisfaction etc.

From a different base, this emerging development approach has also grown out of the pragmatic problem of carrying out development programs in rural undeveloped parts of the world. Starting with Rapid Rural Analysis (RRA) in villages for which there was no formal data available, this movement morphed into a variety of types and processes including Participatory Action Research (PAR). PAR seeks to both understand the world and change it, collaboratively and reflectively. An alternative to positivism in science, this emergent research tradition of 60 years emphasizes principles of collective inquiry and experimentation grounded in experience and social history.

Within a PAR process (Reason and Bradbury write) 'communities of inquiry and action evolve and address questions and issues that are significant for those who participate as co-researchers' Robert Chambers has been a leading advocate of this new way of approaching development, which is about shifting the emphasis from products and services to that of people (Figure 2.7). However there is not an established body of knowledge, such as exists for building solutions to 'Tame' problems in

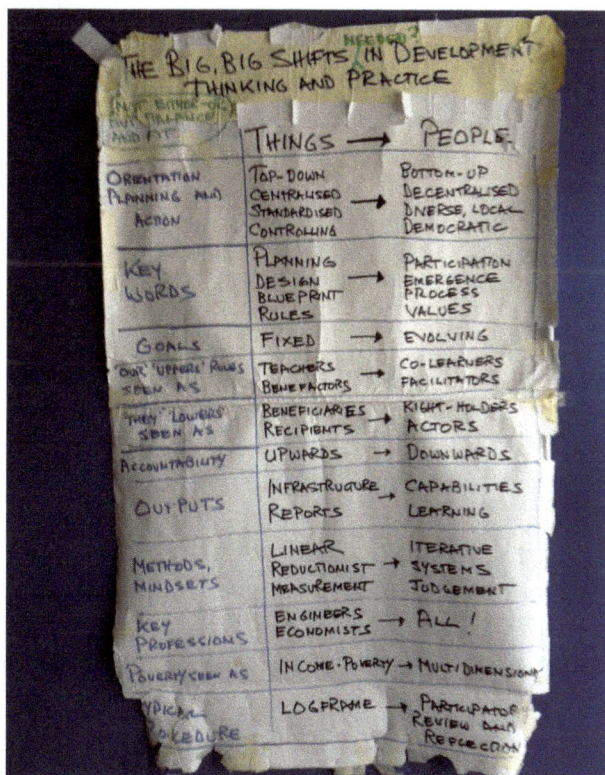

Figure 2.7 Robert Chambers: The changing development paradigm. Photo of poster Robert Chambers used in his training workshops.

complicated situations, to working within this new paradigm, even if the need is becoming more understood. For instance, the recently published (Feb 2017) UN New Urban Agenda mentions the word 'participation' in 32 of the 160 functional paragraphs.

> *Para 41. We commit ourselves to promoting institutional, political, legal and financial mechanisms in cities and human settlements to broaden inclusive platforms, in line with national policies, that allow meaningful participation in decision-making, planning and follow-up processes for all, as well as enhanced civil engagement and co-provision and co-production.*[2]

As I found in northern New South Wales, whilst good in theory, transferring the theory into action has proven to be a challenge. It is far easier to make statements about participation, collaboration, inclusion and empowerment than actually do it. There is a gap between the image and the reality. However it is the process of working collaboratively in the design process to solve Tame problems (outputs) that helps build stronger links between individuals. Thus it seems a useful conceptual development model for the social age.

The concept of design – an iterative process to achieve a desired product or state – seems relevant and useful for growth and change to occur. It might be known in a variety of terminologies (design, Action Learning, Action Research) but fundamentally it means a process of searching for the ideal, whilst answering multiple criteria based in the real world.

To help in this design process there is another useful tool that provides a structural framework with which to work. As important as the Gantt chart (invented in 1910 by Henry Gantt) for project managers, the LogFrame is the equivalent for those working with Wicked problems in complex systems.

It was in the later part of the 1960s that the US development agency USAID was struggling with the challenge of how to solve a Wicked problem such as ours, and the limitation of only being able to design and build projects and programs such as digging wells and instigating health programs. Their solution revolutionised the approach to aid programs for it described a useful way to create a link between a vision or goal and an action or output. This was the invention of the LogFrame.

LogFrames

The LogFrame (Figure 2.8) provides a link between a concrete activity (which we can control) and a desired effect within the broader system (which we can influence at best). As a framework based on logic it overcomes the limitations of acting out of ideology or belief, but does not negate the role of culture.

Outcome
Strategy
Output
Action

Figure 2.8 The LogFrame. An internationally used program logic tool to describe the linkages between various components of purposeful endeavour.

The LogFrame provides a format that establishes a logical relationship between an Activity (space program) an Output (such as moon landing) and an Outcome (such as Americans feel good about themselves), the Outcome being the desired effect within a complex system. In between the Output and Outcome is the Strategy, which in simple terms is the thinking behind the decision as to what to do.

The LogFrame helps provide a link between a desired outcome (which exists within the complex system) and an actionable, achievable output. It is a process that at one end has the statement of a broad aim, vision or goal and at the other a specific action that needs to be taken to achieve it. It provides a logical rationale for carrying out actions as opposed to following convention, acting on a good idea or waiting for fate. If all that one can do is design an output, the strategy or thinking is all-important.

The process is sometimes also known by the metaphor Splash and Ripple: all a person can do is an action (pick up a rock and drop it into the lake). This results in an output (the splash). Depending on how well chosen and directed the stone is (strategy), the ripples will achieve the desired outcome in the broader system (the reeds to wave, the frog spawn to hatch, etc).

Whilst the words to describe each of the components of the metaphor often change, the functions remain the same. Thus words such as goal, outcome, vision are often interchangeable for a specific idea; that is, a desired end state within the broader system. Equally there are different words used for each level of logic. The different words in each level of the LogFrame are just some of the common terms used for the same aspect of the framework. In its simplest form the LogFrame comprises just four lines, each line or level having a logical relationship between the one above and the one below.

When completing a LogFrame, each level has to be self-contained with only one element. Words such as through, by, to, and with, are linking words that span different elements between the levels. The heavy line separating Strategies from Outputs indicates the limits of what one can physically do. In other words, the limiting factor of any Action is an Output.

The era of the technical professional has been defined by the capacity to create and produce tangible goods and defined services at a rate never before achieved in the known history of the world. It has defined modern humans' existence as profoundly as did the church in the thirteenth century.

In our current era of transition, we are confronted with a culture that embraces ideas of change, whilst a changing natural and social environment demands ideas of both sustainability and adaptability, inclusion and co-operation, the latter being components of a complex not complicated system.

My understanding of sustainability was shifting from ideas relating to outputs to something far more 'complex'. Something like a sustainable decision, which is perversely both an output and an outcome, seems best achieved when all stakeholders are part of the decision-making process. This then became my new challenge. As a designer, how might I best assist others be part of the decision-making, or design process? The answer that emerged for me was to design processes that would help groups of people work together through the Action Learning/ Design process. That in itself became a personal learning process.

To be effective in the emerging development paradigm, we need more people to be comfortable with the iterative, Action Learning/ Design process to help individual change and growth. The emerging social age provides not just an opportunity but an imperative for more people to become part of the design process. We need more people to think. And to do this it requires more people to work together in the design process (Figure 2.9).

Figure 2.9 The writing on the wall. The difference between acceptance of something and designing for a desired future.

What this led to is my own personal logic model (Figure 2.10).

Goal	A place where all sentient beings etc. ....
Strategy	Strengthen the nodes and linkages of our social system.
Outputs	Design and implement facilitated workshops
Actions	Practice and learn from carrying out as many facilitated workshops as possible

Figure 2.10. My personal Logic model to achieve the desired goal.

The Strategy is that if more people have the opportunity to participate in the design process they might develop and grow as individuals, and doing it together will help develop the capacity for stronger linkages. In other words, strengthen the human system in both the I and We development zones.

Summary

In our current transitional period there is a significant desire by many to be involved in the decisions that affect them. In the same period, a different way of looking at the world describes the characteristics of complex systems, an observation that can help structure development theory. A conceptual tool that is highly relevant to successfully working in complex systems is Action Learning/Research. The Action Research/ Design process is a significant contribution to the world's development. It has driven most of the innovations that have contributed to *Homo sapiens'* success in the world. Key new observations relevant for today and the challenge of creating a plan for the given design problem, are (1) acknowledging the existence of complex systems, and how they are different to complicated systems, and (2) recognising that Action Learning/Design or evidence-based decisions is a useful tool for humanity. The combination of these observations is that the stated goal of 'a world in which all sentient beings... etc.' will not be achieved if viewed as a difficult but essentially Tame problem. We have to view it as a Wicked problem to be solved within an understanding of a complex system. Design in the new paradigm requires both a different process and different understanding of success to traditional design problems.

At its core, it requires approaching the design problem as something that will evolve out of a strong system that comprises strong nodes and linkages, not as something that with enough research we can go out and create. That requires individuals learning through being engaged in developing the solutions to the problems that confront us.

The Machine Age was built on the basis of science and technology. The underlying disci-pline of the Social Age is psychology. Just as the wheel can be used for a tank or an ambulance, psychology can be used to either empower and help others develop and grow, or control and stunt others. To survive, for us as humans to develop and grow as a species will require all to be part of the process of change

To achieve the goal of a strong human system means providing the opportunities for everybody to experience and be part of the Action Learning/Design process. As this then became my own value set, I saw that the logic model to achieve the desired outcome gave me two possible outputs. The first is to advocate that more people are involved in the process of designing the solutions to problems that affect them, and the second is to become a skilled enabler in the Action Learning/Design process.

CHAPTER 3

Values, power and structure

As well as providing a new approach to individual change and growth, the technical/professional era has provided many with previously unheard-of opportunities for both individual empowerment, control, and choice.

One of the legends concerning the heroes of the modern movement was how they broke down the taboos and cultural norms regarding what houses and the built environment should be like. It was right and proper to be a disrupter. From Harry Siedler's monumental battle with Woollahra Council (the house he'd designed for his mother didn't look like a house as defined by the Council) to Ayn Rand's fictional hero Howard Roark (In which the protagonist blew up the building that was not constructed to his design), the underlying message was the legitimacy of the designer to have control and choice in the expression of built form and creation of space. These designers wanted to break free of the constraints and prohibitions imposed by the establishment holders of taste and propriety. They saw a new future in designing spaces and places that embraced a new optimism and all that it might offer for humanity. They espoused their right to express their own ideas and showcase them in the built form.

At an everyday level, the railways and the later development of the car have enabled many people unprecedented levels of control and choice. More opportunities to commute from home to work, allowing many far greater control and choice over both their living and work spaces than in any traditional culture. The car has provided unbelievable opportunities for travel and social mobility, and even who you meet with. Take for example, Ed Kienholz's work *Back Seat Dodge 38*, an installation comprising two intertwined figures on the rear seat of a car in which the whole of the front seat section had been sliced out. Similarly an advertisement for a Model T Ford shows a couple having a picnic in the countryside. On the bottom of the advertisement in large letters are the words Free and Independent – free and independent to be with the person of your choice in a location you choose. In terms of power, think of all the car advertisements that promise prospective owners more power. Contemporary Australian suburbs continue to provide immense opportunities for people to explore their dreams, express their view of the world, and to have control and choice over their personal domain. Owning a car enables people to access cheaper land on the periphery of the city. How one then views the kind of housing available, choices provided by volume builders, trade-offs in regard to distance to services, are all characteristic of decisions being made in a complex system.

Frames and framing

A helpful insight to the challenges of working in complex systems can be gained from the idea of *frames and framing*, part of the emerging social development lexicon (Q 3.1).

Framing in the social sciences *refers to a set of concepts and theoretical perspectives on how individuals, groups, and societies organise, perceive, and communicate about. Framing is commonly used in* sociology, psychology, *and* political science.[1]

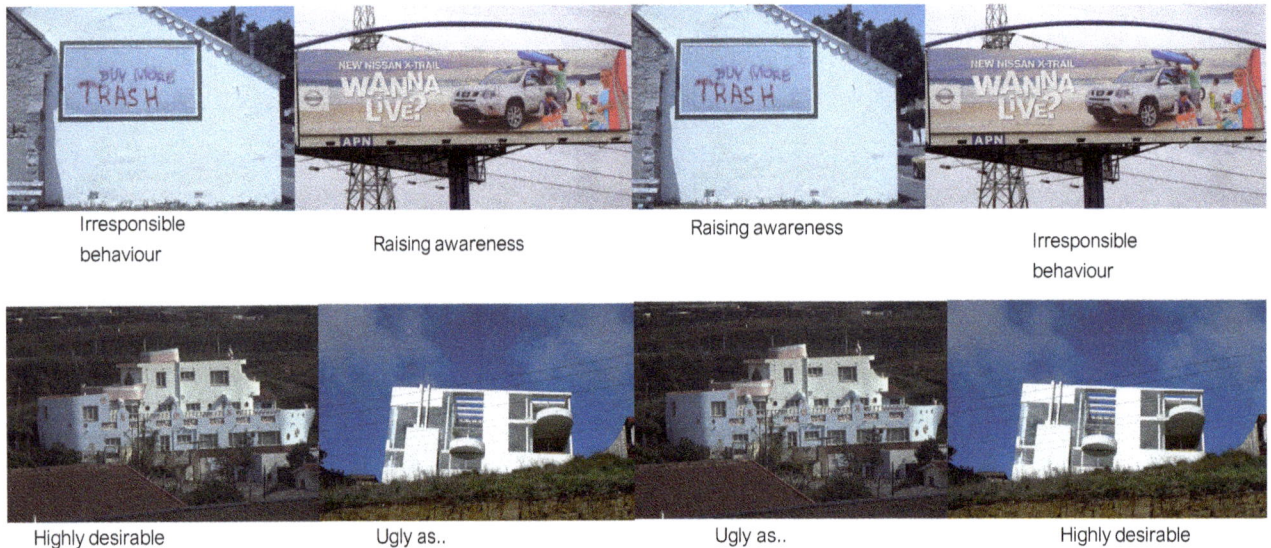

| Irresponsible behaviour | Raising awareness | Raising awareness | Irresponsible behaviour |

| Highly desirable | Ugly as.. | Ugly as.. | Highly desirable |

Figure 3.1 How people view the same thing is often very different

The theory is that different people might look at the same thing but interpret what they see in different ways (Figure 3.1). In other words, individuals or groups of individuals see the world in particular or unique ways.

To most this might be self-evident, for we can probably acknowledge that even those closest to us have a different view on the world in some respects. For example a tobacco industry executive might acknowledge that, in his view, his perception of reality is right, there are others with a different view, even if in his mind they have the wrong view. What this means is that when using a design tool such as the LogFrame, the logic will always be dependent on the cultural frame of reference of the creator of the framework. Thus while the LogFrame is a really useful design tool, its widespread implementation has not provided the kind of development results hoped for when initially created and later widely adopted. In simple terms it's because either (or both) the values of those that develop the plan are not the same as those for whom the plan is developed, or simply that whilst there might be agreement, it is not owned by the one implementing the action. There is often consensus around the vision or goal (healthier people living longer lives, for instance). The problems arise when we consider

the strategy: how to achieve the goal which in turn leads to determining what concrete, tangible product or service to create.

For example, consider the following five scenarios each starting with the same goal: 'Having a happy family'. In each case the logic is a reflection of the ideology, frame or values of the person developing the plan.

Water engineer: Achieve your Goal of a happy family by having easy access to fresh water (Strategy). This requires a reticulated water system (Output) and you should volunteer to dig the trenches this afternoon.

Health professional: To achieve your Goal of a happy family requires that they have access to a good health service (Strategy). This means having a doctor in town (Output) and you should sign this petition for one right now. (Action)

Soft drink salesman: Achieve your Goal of a happy family by drinking our product (Strategy). This requires having a bottle in your fridge (Output) and you should buy some right now. (Action)

Music teacher: To achieve your Goal of having a happy family requires that they are entertained (Strategy). Thus you should play the piano for them tonight (Output) and an action you could take is to attend piano lessons today.

Politician (elected representative): To achieve your Goal of having a happy family requires them to be well represented (Strategy). Thus you should elect me to represent you (Output) and an action you could take is to vote for me today.

In each case the logic works well, but when the frame is set by somebody else with different values, the logic does not necessarily stack up. Sometimes they coincide, near enough, but often they are at odds with our own reality.

Nowadays a common approach by policy makers, project managers and decision makers to this problem is to undertake research into people's values to ensure that they are incorporated into a decision. In much the same way, postmodernism with its ethos of multivalency suggested a way forward. But the Action Learning process is still held by the professional making the decisions. It begs the question: if it's OK for a variety of values to be expressed in a decision such as the built environment, why not enable the people with those values to express them themselves?

If genuine learning and development is going to occur through the Action Learning process, the logic has to be owned by those who are going to implement the action. It is this learning process that has contributed significantly to the historically unprecedented increase in life expectancy and general wellbeing of the human population. The logic model is that to achieve the desired outcome, a strategy would be for more people to have the opportunity to experience the Action Learning process. At a day-to-day level this is not as easy as it might seem.

Power

Power is central to how change occurs – or not. Technical professionals use logic, specialist expertise and an understanding of meeting proce-

dures to ensure their view of reality is implemented. Other examples of power that people use to implement their values, their frame of reference, over others include:

1. physical power (very common in medieval times)
2. social rank (imperative in 1750)
3. organisational or institutional rank (military, today's corporations and government departments)
4. ability to stay awake and talk the longest (often used in ecovillage-politics)
5. talk the most eloquently (nineteenth-century politics)
6. number of followers (gang/political party/size of department)
7. technical expertise & rational argument (common nowadays from professionals)
8. charisma/looks/charm
9. financial power (access to advertising, etc.)
10. representational power (politicians)
11. race
12. gender.

There are many others, and many also intersect. I invite you to add to the list.

An ecovillage is an intentional, traditional or urban community that is consciously designed through locally owned, participatory processes in all 4 dimensions of sustainabiity (social, culture, ecology, economy into a whole systems design) to regenerate its social and natural environment.[2]

One way in which power is exercised that you may not have included is found in the work of Steven Karpman. In 1958 Karpman identified two very different ways in which people affect power. These are power as a Victim and power as a Rescuer. Also featuring the Persecutor (which can take the form of any of the above), these two types of power are commonly expressed in modern welfare states. The Rescuer gains power through taking the high moral ground, or advocating for someone else. This is compared to enabling the Victim to speak for themselves. People playing victim ('poor me' syndrome) are also a component of Karpman's Drama Triangle. Karpman explains how genuine and real development can only occur when people step out of the drama triangle.

Whilst there are numerous ways in which people exercise power, there is an equally infinite variety of things that people do with it, and why they do it. A classic observation by Sherry

Arnstein was articulated in her paper of 1968 entitled 'A Ladder of Citizen Participation' in the *Journal of the American Planning Association.*

The ladder (Figure 3.2) set out nine steps between manipulation and citizen control to describe the relationship between government (those with the mandate, or power to make decisions) and citizens. Arnstein's paper also documented contemporary examples illustrating how governments and those with financial and relationship power exercised their values over others with less power through sham engagement processes; that is, communication techniques that are in practice tokenism and manipulative. In particular, she examined the promotion of values held by the technical professionals who hold power across all sectors of society, whether within or external to government.

Of course, there are times when it is necessary for those with power to be dictatorial, but that is different to phoney inclusion. Peter Sandman, known for his work on Risk Communication, identified that in considering Risk and Concern there is only one situation where people actively want to be told what to do. That is when you are in a situation of extreme danger and you are very concerned about it (such as when on an aeroplane and an engine catches fire). In all other instances (High Risk/Low Concern; Low Risk/High Concern; Low Risk/Low Concern) you want to be part of a discussion. You want to express your view of the situation, your values, your frame of reference. Gilbert Brenson Lazan identifies that those with power and authority to exercise power legitimately in times of crisis will often use the crisis as a justification to extend their power well after the real crisis has mitigated. His suggestion is that once people are out of immediate danger, in a tent and with food, they want to be talking. In his view, this is generally three days after a crisis event.

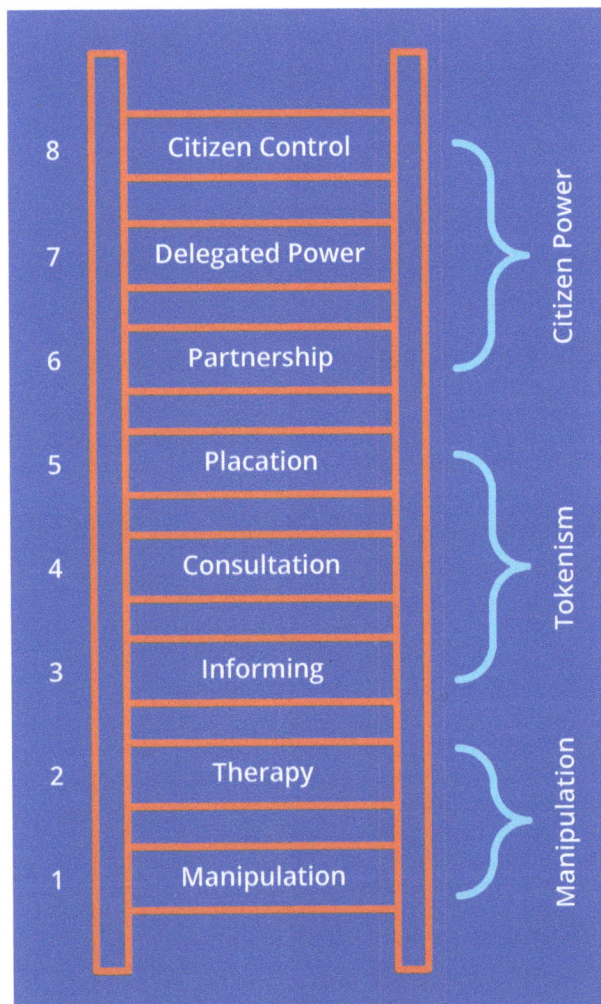

Figure 3.2 The Ladder of Citizen Participation by Sherry Arnstein. The conceptual ladder provides a spectrum of how those with power engage with those without power, ranging from manipulation through to handing over power.

They might be traumatised, they might have all kinds of concerns, but equally they have to be talking to each other, helping each other go through the process of grief and loss with their peers. It is more than merely being provided with a service.

Control and choice (that is, personal power in making a decision) is a critical component linking change and its impact on the broader system. Consider moving house. Compare the effect of moving house because you have bought a new one to moving house because you have been evicted. Much of the effect on you, any potential outcomes from such a stressful event, will hinge on whether it has been because you've chosen it compared with it being outside of your control.

Running workshops for groups of people to work together and express their own world views and ideas to complex problems requires new theory, tools and techniques.

Developing the strategy

Within the context of a facilitated workshop for a number of participants (who will, by definition, have diverse views) I have found two frameworks very useful. The first structural framework is a workshop process that results in a group creating their own LogFrame. The LogFrame fits the idea of bottom-up development, that is where a group has the imprimatur to develop both the strategy and the projects or programs (outputs) to achieve a desired outcome.

Within the English language, there can be more than one meaning for the word *plan*. As well as being both a noun and a verb, two distinct types of plan are strategic and operational. Unfortunately, like the words *output* and *outcome*, there is often confusion. The phrase *strategic planning* is sometimes used by those wanting to make out that what they are doing is somehow more important than mere planning. However as with so much in our complex social environment, whilst there are times when the difference can be murky, at the extremes there are clear differences. I find it useful to describe the difference as follows: Strategic planning answers the question why, Operational planning

the question how. Thus this framework works really well to answer the strategic planning component of the Action Learning/Design cycle.

By bottom-up, I mean the situation where to achieve a desired outcome, the intention is to enable participants develop a logical basis to implement a specifc concrete tangible output that they are able to carry out (that is, create a strategic plan). The desired outcome might be something that they have created themselves using a visioning activity, or it may be something that they have been given by others and are willing enough to work towards. The concrete, tangible output that participants decide on has to be logical for them, and within their capacity to implement.

When working with a group, I will use questions based on those developed by the Institute of Cultural Affairs' Technology of Participation (ToP) process (Figure 3.3). The usefulness of the sequence of questions is that the answers naturally make a LogFrame and thus a strategic plan.

	Questioning sequence for 'Bottom - Up' development
1	What is the vision?
3	What are the current underlying blockages to the vision?
4	What concrete tangible outputs could you do to overcome the blockages?
5	What activities do you need to accomplish these outputs (wall chart)

Figure 3.3 Questioning sequence to develop a logical relationship between a concrete action and a desired outcome

It is easier for people to define what the blockages are than to set out what strategy we should use. By asking the group to identify the underlying blockages to their particular vision, it provides the opportunity to ask what concrete tangible outputs could that group produce to overcome the blockage. Once those have been identified, a series of actions can be developed to make the designed output happen. This process of swapping positives and negatives is a useful way to explore all kinds of things. People often express a desired outcome as a problem, which can be reframed from a negative into a positive (Figure 3.4). Within an architectural framework, this is akin to the Figure/ground drawings often done to see the situation from a different perspective.

Problem	Vision or goal
Economic Collapse	We have a stable and useful economic system
Peak Oil	We are no longer dependent on oil for a great lifestyle
Global Water Crisis	There is plenty of clean water for all
Species Extinction	Our bio-diversity is strengthened and maintained
Rapid Climate Change	We can thrive in an unpredictable climate

Figure 3.4 Reframing problems into visions

When it comes to writing a report or funding proposal, the blockages can be reframed from a negative to a positive and called a strategy. For example, an underlying blockage to *having an oil-free lifestyle* might be *the power of the fossil fuel lobby* and thus the strategy becomes *reducing the power of the fossil fuel lobby*. A further variation to this concept is a questioning sequence designed for conservation rather than change.

1. What do you love?
2. What are the threats?
3. What can we do to overcome the threats?
4. Action planning.

When working within a government organisation, I often find that the vision or outcome has already been set. It might be in a project document or a corporate plan. In this instance it is sufficient to bring the stated vision to the awareness of the group, and then proceed with the subsequent questions. The important element is that the participants have the capacity and autonomy to achieve the vision within their own frame of reference.

The second framework is more a useful process that fits within the second of my personal actions, that is, to advocate for those who will be affected by a decision to be part of the decision-making process.

In contemporary society there are individuals and groups that hold legitimate institutional power. These people and groups are often referred to as either leaders or decision makers. If amongst them there is a desire (or often a directive, to comply with Human Rights or comply with local requirements) to engage others in the development of that project. The critical parts are for the project owners to the project parameters in terms of negotiables and not-negotiables and the project team to analyse stakeholders according to stake and power.

To achieve this I use the following series of questions as a form of participatory analysis.

1. 'Which individuals or groups will be affected by this project when it is finished?' (the stakeholders)

2. 'What are the "negotiables" and what are the 'non-negotiables' about the project.' The Not Negotiables are either because of existing policy, have already been decided by the group, or are a stipulation by the Project Owner.

3. Participants rank (vertically) the stakeholders according to their "stake" in how the negotiables are resolved (within the context of the non-negotiables).

4. Participants rank (horizontally) the stakeholders according to the power they have to affect the final product.

Figure 3.5 The Communication Spectrum, derived from Arnstein's Ladder of Participation. It helps project managers understand how they might build or strengthen the social system, and avoid inadvertently depleting it.

This participatory analysis results in every stakeholder being in one of four quadrants: high stake/high power; high stake/low power; high power/low stake; low stake/low power.

This process can also be viewed at https://www.youtube.com/watch?v=1D95bHNgHiI.

Using the communication spectrum (Figure 3.5), I interpret that those that have a high stake/high power are the collaborators on the project. For those with a high stake/low power it is necessary

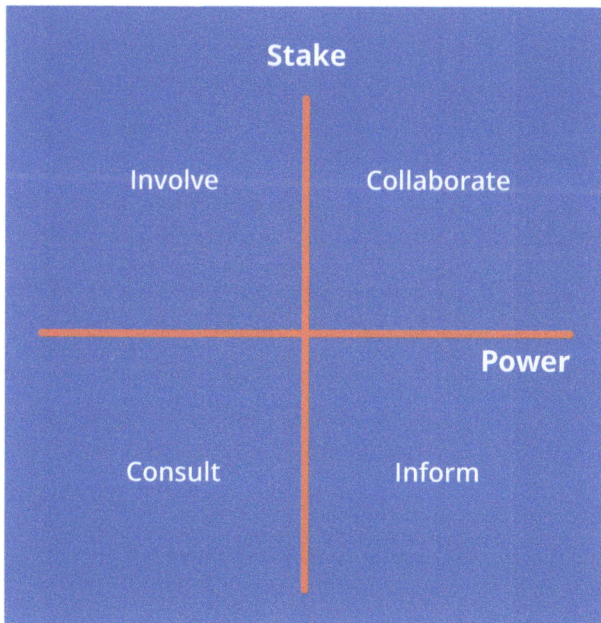

Figure 3.6 An interpretation of a stakeholder analysis carried out by first ranking stakeholders by 'stake' in a project and program (top to bottom), followed by grading the formal 'power' (L-R) each stakeholder has to influence the project or program.

for the collaborators to at least involve them in the resolution of the negotiables, and often collaborate on specifics of the project. Because we are naturally seduced by those with power, project teams often give those with power but low stake greater say than they need to have. Whilst there may be nothing wrong with that, negating the opportunities for those with less power in society to determine answers to problems that affect them again undermines the potential for learning and developing social capital (Figure 3.6).

Thus there are two structural frameworks that I often use. The first is the LogFrame, which can be completed by a group using the ToP questioning process. The second is the stakeholder engagement planning framework. In essence, each of these frameworks roughly correspond to whether the project (that is the concrete tangible product) is *bottom up* or *top down*.

However, as complexity is never simple, it is often the case that there are times in which a project sits in one area, and at other times the other. For instance, consider a project that starts with a very general and open question about neighbourhood development. It might be about achieving the goal of good education for kids (bottom up). This might translate into carrying out a feasibility study for a new school (top down) which coincides with a group looking at curricula (bottom up) etc. The result is an ongoing conversation that has its own trajectory

Top Down Community Engagement

Usually starting from a stated output; eg policy, program, report.

People actively participating in projects and programs that have meaning to them.

Bottom Up Community Initiated

Usually starting with a desired outcome eg: healthy people.

Figure 3.7 Most projects and programs comprise a mixture of top-down and bottom-up initiatives. If the desire is to strengthen the system, each requires its own process.

(Figure 3.7). The conversation not only moves, but there are different perspectives constantly being expressed over the term of the project life. How those conversations are held is a critical component of success.

ORID and transcendence

ORID is one of the more unfortunate acronyms I've come across, not least because it is so useful as a concept. Conceptually I feel it is very similar to Strategic Questioning by Fran Peavey. Both tools provide a questioning model or sequence

that helps others think through a problem in a logical sequence. ORID stands for:

1. Objective
2. Reflective
3. Interpretative
4. Decisional

Thus the first questions are along the lines of 'What's been happening?' Then the questions become reflective, such as 'How do you feel about that?', leading into interpretive questions such as 'Why do you think that is?' and finally 'What are you going to do now?'

I know people who can develop such questions on the fly, but if I use it in a workshop setting I always have to plan them out beforehand. In fact, I often use the examples provided in the *Art of Focused Conversation* (edited by R. Bruce Stanfield, 2000) as inspiration. The underlying theory is to help the other, often the individual, to work through the problem-solving process themselves, utilising their own experience and their own strategies to achieve the goals they want. The questioning process is that of one person helping the thought process of another. When people have to think through a process, they change and grow as an individual. This concept of transcendence is also applicable in a group setting, not just an individual. The difference is that the tools and techniques used will be different

Conceptually, the ORID process is similar to the diverge/converge model of transcendental decision making invented by Sam Kaner (Figure 3.8), apparently with the help of some architect friends.

Kaner maintains that the dialogue process is essential to achieve the kind of neat solutions to complex problems that are desired. At first glance this can sound contrary to the statement that *for every complex problem there is a simple solution, and it's wrong*. The distinction lies in the shifting of perceptions that participants make

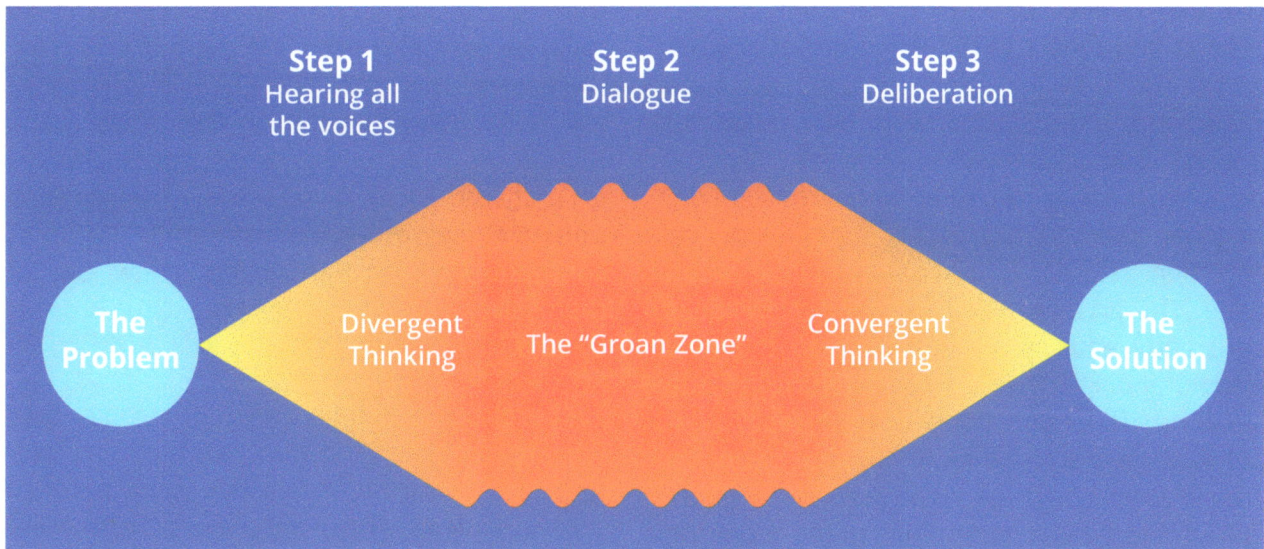

Figure 3.8 An interpretation by the author of Sam Kaner's Diverge/Converge concept.

not only through listening to each other, but also by having the opportunity to develop their own collective answer to the issue. It is the understanding that people change their thinking after listening to others, especially when jointly trying to develop a concrete tangible product. It is applicable whether carried out by an individual in the privacy of their own computer, or for a group of people. When it is with a group of people, individuals might initially be supporting solution A, or solution B. It is through the process of dialogue and deliberation that a completely different solution (e.g. $\triangle^2$) emerges.

An early structured example of this process of transcendence is the Delphi process. In its original form it was a forecasting method invented by the Rand Corporation for the US military in the early 1960s. In this instance a group of military experts were each sent a questionnaire asking them their professional recommendation to a complex problem. The results were collected, de-identified, and sent back to all participants. This time the participants were asked if they wanted to alter their initial suggestions based on the recommendations made by their colleagues. This process is carried out at least twice, sometimes up to four times, the result being insights from a collective thought process, not just that of an individual.

The diverge/converge model describes three parts of a process that can lead to transformative or transcendental solutions. The first step might be called hearing all the voices. In traditional design parlance, this includes getting the brief, understanding all the parameters such as budget, context constraints, legislative framework etc. as well as generating ideas for a possible solution. Transformative solutions emerge not from procedural activities, but from ideas. These ideas might be only relatively innovative in themselves, but are created and perceived to be innovative by those involved in the problem-solving process. In many instances they are not so much ideas as positions. But they are still expressions of a solution, albeit unlikely to be acceptable to all.

The more limited the life experiences and technical knowledge of the individuals or group, the more limited the ideas. This leads to one of the greatest differences between the era of the professional/technical and the emerging social age. The professional/technical age revered the ideas of the professional/technical. The social age recognises the legitimacy of all ideas.

From this initial analysis and expression of ideas, the groan zone is a period of uncertainty and often stress. Either as an individual or as a group member, trying to develop a solution that reflects and meets all the different parameters and values is always uncomfortable. This is the nature of the transformative or transcendental process, and occurs either when an individual designer is trying to find an optimum solution, or when there is a group of people working together. Sam Kaner describes it as the groan zone. The art is to keep it playful. New ideas constantly emerge that respond to the new understandings that individuals have of the situation. There are times when a really neat solution seems to be emerging, but suddenly the parameters change. Or an assumption taken is found to be erroneous. And so more playing around is required. Eventually, a solution to the problem will emerge, a solution that on the surface might seem to be almost simple — something that might elicit the comment of being obvious. However, it will not be a simplistic solution. It will be like the Rose Window in Chartres Cathedral: many layers of meaning embodied into something that on the surface might look just like another stained glass window. Or how the shells of the Opera House were eventually resolved. As mentioned, the process is just as applicable for a single designer working in isolation as it is when a group of people are working together. The difference is how that group works together, the relationships between the individuals, and how the power dynamics are resolved.

Facilitated Participatory Design

This emerging design field is achieved by aligning the concept of group facilitator with Participatory Action Research or Design, resulting in Facilitated Participatory Design (FPD). The role of the designer in FPD is to create a safe space that enables people with different viewpoints and world views to both express their ideas and listen to others.

An important part of the workshop design is developing questions for the group, but the frame of these questions is different to doing a survey to find out people's preferences prior to making a decision. The questions are designed to (a) be useful for others to solve the problem themselves, (b) enable dialogue with others who will be similarly impacted by the decision, and (c) to come to a common understanding based on a shared frame of reference. The common understanding emerging from an FPD process contributes to the participants' knowledge of themselves and their relationship to the broader system.

To be effective with a group of people, Sam Kaner maintains that the process has to be face-to-face in real time. It also has to be between those people who have the power to implement the solution. Thus whilst the process is eminently scaleable, and is applicable when considering the structure of a large engagement project or working through a small detail with a few stakeholder participants, to be sustainable the solution reached has to be owned by those with the power to support it. By definition those will be those with power through culturally accepted means (such as being a public servant, or elected authority), and those with power through other means.

Summary

To summarise, there is growing awareness and desire for participatory development to occur. There are a number of problems that inhibit its effective take-up and success. The first is simply that those with power in society (however it is gained or expressed, either consciously or unconsciously) naturally want their frame of reality dominate any participatory process. This is most often achieved through convincing, in whatever way works for them, that their idea is best. Sometimes this extends to even manipulating the evidence to achieve outcomes that benefit themselves. The second is that it is only more recently (that is, in approximately the last 60 years) that there has been understanding about how people might best work together inclusively when there is no hierarchical or institutional power structure. Together with the LogFrame and Stakeholder Analysis frameworks, the Action Learning/Design and diverge/ converge concepts provide considerable scope to helping groups work together and find transformational solutions to problems. It is highly scaleable, and flexible.

Additionally there are a number of question series that I find can help others work together and overcome some of the hurdles of participatory development. The following are techniques that I find useful on a regular basis, in all kinds of situations. Some are more useful where there are larger groups of people, some more useful for smaller. However those for larger can often be modified to work with small numbers of people, and equally vice versa.

Some theoreticians and practitioners are most cautious about recommending any kind of participatory development methodology, for instance Bob Dick invites the reader of his

manual to disregard the instructions. Reflecting on my own experience of learning how to facilitate groups and undertake FPD, the process is much the same as learning any other design field. Long hours spent reading and attending training workshops. Tentative and naive first steps, ideally in a supportive environment. When it came to trying things out, initial attempts were highly derivative. It is only later, through experience and reflection, that a personal style evolves.

Nowadays I find the most successful approach to the design process itself is to work in real time with the project owner. This can either be using a whiteboard, but often just as successfully carried out using a screen share tool and a phone. As an Action Learner, I am constantly changing my practice. What follows are tools and techniques that I currently often use, or have found useful in the past.

CHAPTER 4

Tools and techniques

As explained in the previous chapters, the structural models I use to help teams or groups of people to work collaboratively together and achieve sustainable decisions are:

1. The Action Learning concept
2. Diverge/Converge concept/ORID
3. Bottom-up framework (LogFrame)
4. Top-down stakeholder analysis framework

In this section I document some of the techniques I use to implement the concepts and models. Many of the techniques can be used for more than one element of each structure. Thus I might use the same technique for a group to collaboratively develop their vision at the beginning of a process as I would use towards the end of a process to reflect on what they have done. The difference is the questions used within the technique. The context is critical, not the technique itself. Having said that, I have roughly grouped the techniques into seven categories.

1. Relationship building
2. Visioning
3. Specialist information
4. Participatory analysis
5. Combination techniques
6. Action planning
7. Asynchronous processes

Almost all (the exception being the poster process) have come my way through either attending other people's workshops or reading about them, mostly from one of two books: J. Pretty, I. Guijit, J. Thompson & I. Scoones, *Participatory Learning and Action : A Trainers Guide*, and R. B. Williams, *More Than 50 Ways to Build Team Consensus*.

Whilst not essentially techniques, two key skills are necessary for implementing any of the techniques.

1. Developing and asking the right questions.
2. Listening (and I've found, even if not listening well, not talking)

The question lies at the centre of every technique. It is what you want the participants to discuss. My experience is that it should be only one question at a time. This helps provide focus to discussions.

There are four types of questions:

- Open
- Closed
- Leading
- Ambiguous

Leading questions are not good for this kind of work. This is where it is a statement dressed up to sound like a question. An example is 'Don't you think owning a house is the best option?'

Ambiguous questions do not assist, and are harder to spot. An example is 'Do people come here often? The answers are dependent on individual interpretation of the word often.

Closed questions need to be used cautiously. These are questions that can only be answered with a yes or no. Generally they should be asked towards the end of a convergent process, when it is a matter of confirmation of what you are hearing. 'I think I'm hearing that there is an agreement to buy a house, is this correct?'

Open questions are those that drive discussion. 'What are your thoughts about buying a house?' Open questions that invite conversation underpin all the techniques.

I have also tried to keep a consistent reference to three types of the decision-making space. These are:

1. small synchronous workshops (that is, up to six people all meeting at the same time)

2. large synchronous workshops (any number beyond six all meeting at the same time)

3. large scale asynchronous processes (large numbers of people engaged in the process but not necessarily meeting together)

Where the instruction is for participants to work in *pairs* it means groups of two. *Small groups* are ideally groups of three, but if indivisible by 3, have one group of either 2 or 4. *Table groups* should be between 4 to 6 people. Any group over six is usually best split into two.

Relationship building

Theory: People work together best when they have developed some trust and understanding about each other. These are four processes I use to help group participants learn a little more about each other as human beings.

Natural objects

This process works best for those who don't know each other very well, and the level of disclosure is low.

Method: Have a number of natural objects in a bag. Offer someone from each table group to pick one. Ask each table group to describe the qualities of their group illustrated in the natural object. After 5 – 10 minutes have each table group report back (15 minutes).

Introductory bingo

An after-lunch activity for a team that has built some level of understanding between the members (Figure 4.1). It is also good for overcoming the after-lunch slump, and accommodating those returning late.

Figure 4.1 - Introduction bingo. A useful relationship builder

Method: Distribute the sheets and instruct the group to find an answer from a different person for every question. The first one to complete the sheet is the winner (15 minutes), Have that person to read out their answers and, depending on time, invite others to do so as well.

Paired intros

Ask everyone to stand, and to find somebody they don't know. Introduce themselves to one another and start a conversation with the words: 'On the way here I was thinking...' (5 minutes). Bring to a close and instruct the group to find a new person they don't know, introduce themselves to each other and start a conversation with 'I've been interested in (topic) since...' (5 minutes). Repeat if required with a third round, and the conversation starting with 'My hopes for this workshop are...'.

I could tell you a story

A flexible way for participants to learn a little more about each other (Told to me by Deb Lange). Ask the group to form pairs. Demonstrate the following with a volunteer. Taking turns, each participant starts a sentence with the phrase 'I could tell you a story about...'. What they add after is something from their own experience, for example, 'the time I was in a tent 10 metres away from a feeding hippo'. Participants do not tell the story, just the theme or idea. After each has given the other about five or six story ideas from their experience, invite each in turn to ask the other to talk about a story that intrigued them.

Visioning

Creating a vision for the future is different to predicting the future. By definition It has to be creative and imaginative, and a product of the right-hand side of the brain. I have four techniques that I use.

Human statues (20–30 minutes)

Ask the group to form small groups. Instruct each group to create a human statue (strike a pose as example) that involves all of their small group. The statue is to illustrate what success would look like (for the focus of their work). If there are any moving parts, the pose can be held for no more than 30 seconds. Advise them

that they will be playing it back to the whole group in 15 minutes' time, and that they are highly recommended to practice somewhere quiet before this time.

Photo language (15–20 minutes)

Use either one of the proprietary packs available (I particularly like the original set from the Catholic Education Office) or make your own set. Spread out about 15–30 of the photos on a large table that can be accessed from all sides. Ask each of the group to choose a photo that best illustrates what success would look like (for the focus of their work). When all have chosen (and more than one can choose the same photo) ask each to describe their vision for the future using the photo as illustration.

Collage (30–40 minutes)

Prepare a good selection of photos cut out from magazines. Form small groups, provide each group with a sheet of flip-chart paper, collection of photos and glue. Instruct them to create a vision for the future using the pictures. When completed, they describe their vision through the collage (Figure 4.2).

Figure 4.2 Collage created from magazine illustrations used to articulate a vision for the future.

Guided visualisation

Pre-prepare a story of about 200 words. The story is to start with the phrase: 'The date is (about seven years ahead of the present) and for various reasons you have not been involved in the project for a number of years and moved away. Over this time you have heard rumours about the project, and how successful it is. When an opportunity arises for you to revisit your old stomping ground, you take it up with alacrity as you'd love to find out what it was now like. You get out of the bus/stop the car/walk into...and see... and meet... and chat with...and make a mental note to remember...you are amazed at what you see... and, full of awe and wonder, you leave to go back home.' It is best to write this the story based on this framework down and rehearse reading it out loud.

At the allocated time in the workshop, advise all in the group to each take a sheet of paper and pen and find somewhere comfortable to sit. Tell them to close their eyes whilst you slowly and clearly read the story. At the end of the story instruct them to silently and without moving from their seat, write down what they saw, heard and felt.

In the first three of these processes I make notes on cards of the words and phrases used by each group as they explain their image. Using these notes I will ask them to undertake a grouping and naming process to develop the key points for the group.

In the last exercise I then ask table groups to create a newsletter from the future that incorporates their individual visions.

Specialist information

Theory: The kinds of topics groups of people are asked to consider and make decisions about are Wicked problems. That is, problems with no absolute right or wrong answer.

Providing information about what others outside the group think about the topic, or how

they have answered a similar question, provides an opportunity for better decision making.

Literature review *(Group time 30 minutes)*

An engaging approach for new information to be provided and a group to make sense of (told to me by Kate Henderson).

This is not an opportunity for the facilitator to state their preferred option, but to provide the range of how others have thought about it.

Process instructions:

1. Pre-prepare about 8 to 12 extracts (usually mined from the internet) of about 200/300 words each (Figure 4.3).

Figure 4.3 Short texts created on a topic as the content of the Literature Review technique.

2. Create a full set for each table group in the workshop. At the time, organise the group into table groups of about 4 –6 (as per the number of pre-prepared sets).

3. Prepare key questions (usually 1–3).

4. Advise that this is a 3-step process, each step about 10 minutes.

5. Step 1: (10 minutes) Ask the participants to each read a minimum of three extracts IN SILENCE, making note of what is said relevant to the three questions.

6. Step 2: (10 minutes) Ask that the table group elect a scribe. Each table participant to provide a synopsis of their notes. Emphasise that this is an opportunity for all at the table to be heard, not the time for debate.

7. Step 3: (10 minutes) Ask that each table group prepare a few words, or a short statement that describes the essence of their answers, which they write in large print on a sheet of A5 paper.

8. Debrief the answers.

Meaningful presentation

(Group time 30 minutes)

A method to improve the retention and understanding of information provided by someone giving a power point presentation.

Theory:

1. Most people can only take in about 5 minutes' worth of information, or 3–5 key points, at a time.

2. At any given time in a presentation of a complex topic, one person knows it already, one is thinking about the dog, one is asleep, one misheard it and for one it's unintelligible, This leaves one out of six for whom that particular point hits the mark.

3. Many people don't like to ask a question in front of a group of more than about 6.

4. This is a method for a presenter to provide new information, but enable sufficient time for participants to genuinely explore the specialist's expertise.

Process instructions:

1. Brief the speaker on the process, particularly that they will only have maximum 5 minutes to talk.

2. Introduce the speaker and the process.

3. After the 5-minute talk, ask each table group to discuss amongst themselves the content and develop the TWO critical questions they need to ask for clarity. (The easy questions will be answered by their peers in this process.)

4. Ask each table in turn for one question, with the speaker answering each one in about 1 to 2 minutes (Figure 4.4).

Figure 4.4 Listening to the expert, prior to developing questions by table group

5. After the two rounds, and if time, ask if there are any more questions. (Usually there aren't.)

Observations on use:

I use this often, especially when the specialist is someone with institutional rank. The greatest challenge is to persuade the speakers that you want them to speak for 5 minutes only. I find that holding up a stop watch on an iPad so that the presenter can see really useful. Have the setting on Stop Watch not Timer.

A variation is a technique called Petcha Kucha. In the official version, it is when people are given 20 seconds for each of 20 PowerPoint slides (total time 6 mins 40 secs). I have never been so strict. The important thing being that presentations are kept short with a just a few PowerPoint slides.

Beware of anybody that says, 'No worries, I've only got a couple of things to say'. This often means that they don't really know what they want to say, or how they are going to say it. If not careful they will waffle on for 20 minutes. I have volunteered to help them practice first, and always say that I will cut them off after 5 minutes.

Poster process

(Group time 30 minutes)

Type: An engaging approach for new information to be provided (3).

Theory:

1. Literate people can read a lot faster than somebody can talk.

2. Participants will always have varying levels of understanding of any complex topic, from novice to better informed than the presenter.

3. This process allows the participants to become co-presenters as they self-select the area of interest relative to the topic.

Process instructions:

This is a three-part process.

1. Pre-prepare about 12 to 20 posters (information often mined from the internet) with pictures and text of about 200/300 words each. Print out at either A1 or A2 on a plotter.

2. Pre-prepare an A4 sheet with a focus question, and the titles of each poster in alphabetical order.

3. Either before the workshop, or at a suitable break, pin up all the posters, allowing at least 3 metres space between each. Sometimes this means using extra screens, or even table tops.

Part 1: Provide each participant with the A4 sheet listing the alphabetical titles. Instruct them to view the posters SILENTLY for 15 minutes. (Figure 4.5)

Figure 4.5 Viewing the posters in The poster process

Part 2: Divide the group into three, called A, B, and C.

Ask those in Group A to each find a poster that they would like to explore further. Once all have identified a poster each, ask those in Groups B and C to join one of their Group A colleagues for a 5-minute discussion. After 5 minutes call the conversations to a halt, and ask those in Group B to choose a poster. Repeat the process. Finish with Group C participants each choosing a poster, and repeat.

Part 3: Follow up

It is usual to follow up this process with some form of whole group sense-making process, such as a Noisy Round Robin.

Observations on use:

I have used this process for numerous types of content, always successfully. I almost always give participants a scoring sheet containing a focus question for them to use to score each poster. Whilst the scoring sheet is of no specific consequence, it helps ensure that participants actually read the poster. It gives a focus to their reading.

Participatory analysis

The scoping part of the Action Learning/Design concept is distinct whilst also very broad. Whilst close to reflecting on the past, the focus is more on exploring what is happening now. A really useful tool that manages to bridge this area is the History Wall, which also helps put the past into context with the present.

Ranking and Scoring are techniques similar to each other that help participants see their collective views on a topic. The relevance of ranking and scoring exercises is that conceptually it addresses two characteristics of complexity.

1. That ideas, issues, concerns, characteristics are on a spectrum from better to worse.

2. That how things are perceived is dependent on the frame of the viewer.

Participatory Ranking and Scoring exercises thus bring to light how different people view the same item (sometimes similarly, sometimes completely differently, often a mixture). More important is that the participants themselves see the breadth of perception.

Line-ups

Type: A form of analysis, derived from and sometimes known as sociometrics.

(Group time 5–15 minutes)

Theory:

Sociometrics is a form of participatory ranking using people themselves. I generally use it in two situations:

1. As introductory ice-breaker activities

2. Where it is necessary to organise participants for a subsequent activity.

Used as an introductory exercise the activity allows the participants to learn a little more about each other.

Instructions:

Advise participants that they need to stand up, and form a line between two points in the room. Whilst specifically depending on the question to be asked, one point is high and the other low. They are to order themselves on the line depending on their answer to the question (Figure 4.6).

Figure 4.6 Discussing where to stand in a sociometric

When used as an introductory exercise I will start with asking a simple, practical question such as 'How far have you travelled to get here today?' Explain that those who have just walked from home across the road will be at the low end, whilst those that had to fly in last night from another country will be towards the high end.

Once ordered, I will ask them to state where they come from and something that they like about that place. Other questions I have used include:

• How long have you been with your organisation? (Just joined at one end, years and years at the other.)

• How many goats do you own? (When in Malawi.)

Observations on use:

In Malawi I was visiting a bore hole that had just been repaired after not functioning for about three years. Being old, white, male etc., I became the instant visiting dignitary and was expected to say something. Rather than that, I asked the assembled villagers to line up according to how much sicker they'd been since the bore hole broke – no sicker at one end, considerably sicker at the other. After translation and lots of instruction there were clearly people at either end. Thus my next question was what do those at each end have in common? The answer made perfect sense. Those that lived near to the broken bore hole had not been any sicker as they also lived close to an adjoining village which had a functioning bore hole. Those that had been sicker lived further away and the closest alternative water source for them was an unprotected river.

On occasion I have also used sociometrics to determine group members. This might be to ensure that those most experienced in a topic are talking with those who are proportionally less experienced. Or that there is a mixture of experience in each subgroup.

Sticker dots

Type: A highly versatile technique, specifically useful for participatory analysis in the scoping part of the process, and the converge part of a diverge/converge process.

Theory:

1. Having a common understanding of the existing situation is often a useful start for a group embarking on problem solving.

2. Originally developed in situations where formal data was not available (e.g., third world villages), it is now recognised that whilst individuals have a portion of knowledge of a topic, collectively they have a lot.

3. By allowing participants to put more than one dot on an items (usually two, sometimes three) it weights the vote which leads to clearer extremes.

Process instructions:

1. Pre-prepare questions on areas that participants are likely to have knowledge of, for example numbers of people using a facility; when they use the facility; what they do in their leisure time etc.

2. Either the group generates the alternatives or they have come from somewhere else. Either way, set them out with sufficient space to allow participants to place their dots on their preferences.

3. Provide fewer sticker dots than options to individuals. This prevents a donkey vote. Instruct participants to use all their dots. Advise that participants can weight their preferences by placing 2 or 3 dots on the ones they think are especially important to them (Figures 4.7, 4.8, 4.9).

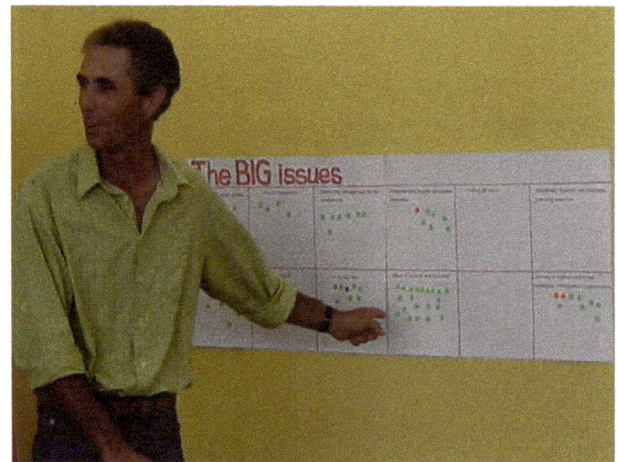

Figure 4.7 A grazier reflecting on the Big Issues he and colleagues felt they faced in the ongoing drought of the early 2000s. I set the board up at a series of three DPI drought field days in SE Queensland. I derived the issues from discussions with various agriculture and social services agencies in the area. One interesting reflection was how each agency felt that their area would be THE big issue.

4. Ask participants to provide their input. This can be in a workshop group, but can equally be in a broad-scale exercise with individuals voting over a period of time.

5. Debrief the answers.

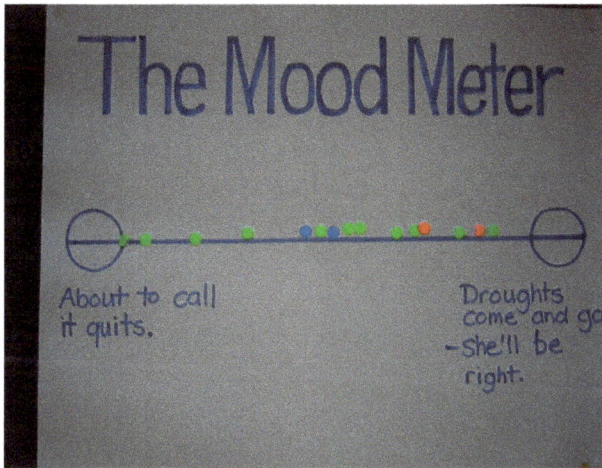

Figure 4.8 Prior to going to the drought field days, I'd heard various stories about the state of outback graziers. These ranged from, 'If the Government doesn't do something soon, there will be a mass walk-off from the land' to 'A bunch of whinging cockies, just because they can't afford a new airplane this year'. Just by simply asking where they would put themselves on the spectrum gave a much more nuanced answer.

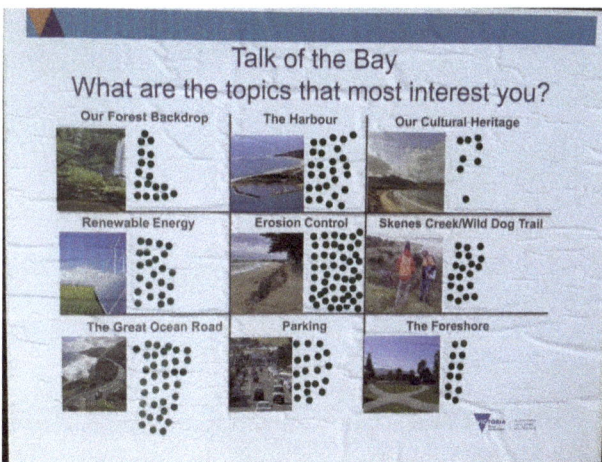

Figure 4.9 The topics of interest to the community attending a listening post at the show.

Observations on use:

Sticker dots are so versatile and so useful that there is a danger of overuse. I often try to deliberately think of alternatives for no other reason than not to use sticker dot voting.

As with everything, mistakes can be made. These include writing the options poorly, so that where to put the dots is ambiguous (is this dot with that one, or the other). In the same vein, it is easy to provide unclear options: to prepare a series of

options and then realise that two (or more) are essentially the same but using different phrasing thus splitting the vote. In a situation where people had a long period of time (a one-day workshop) to place their dots, I made the mistake in a quiet moment of totalling up the dots already placed. This caused confusion for those coming later. One of the great benefits of sticker dots is that the end result is clearly visible to all. The downside is that there is the potential for group think. (I noticed where my manager put her dot, and she is potentially watching where I put mine.) A tactic that I have found to work well is for people to first vote individually on small sheets containing the questions. These sheets are then distributed to everyone in the group with the instruction that they are to place sticker dots on the large (public) sheet in accordance with what is on the sheet they have been given. In this way, voting is secret and the group results are still immediately visible for all to see. It also keeps the power of the vote in the domain of the participants. Transparency of vote counting is not obscured by the facilitator or a select few participants left to count the votes and report back.

Venn diagrams

(Group time 20–30 minutes)

A fundamental component of development in the social realm is relationships. Venn diagramming is a useful mechanism to allow people to map groups and their relationships with each other.

Process instructions:

Prepare a number of different-coloured, different-sized roundels.

Ask the group to generate a list of stakeholders with an interest in the community or project. Using the Card Storming technique is often useful.

Have the group rank the stakeholders according to the power they have in the community or project. This might result in some with a similar level of power, which is OK.

Write the names of the two most powerful stakeholders onto two different-coloured but the largest sized roundels. Write the names of the others onto gradually decreasing sized roundels.

Starting with the two largest roundels, ask the group how much agreement they have in terms of worldview or values. Once decided, go to the next in turn, asking where they would best fit on the diagram. The discussions amongst the participants in deciding where the roundels should fit can be really useful. When completed, take a photo and redraw in the report (Figure 4.10).

Observations on use:

A small but not insignificant observation is that participants often get power and stake confused. I find it necessary to be quite firm about ensuring that there is consistency in the ranking of the stakeholders. Generally, it is power that is the more useful.

History Wall

This is sometimes known as Journey Wall.

(Group time 30–40 minutes)

A useful starter for a workshop to map the activities of the recent past.

Theory:

It is rare for a participatory process to start as if the context were brand new. There have almost always been activities undertaken by the particular group of individuals, or ones relevant to the particular geographic community. Acknowledging this is one level of understanding; fleshing out what that history might be leads to a far richer understanding and experience for all concerned.

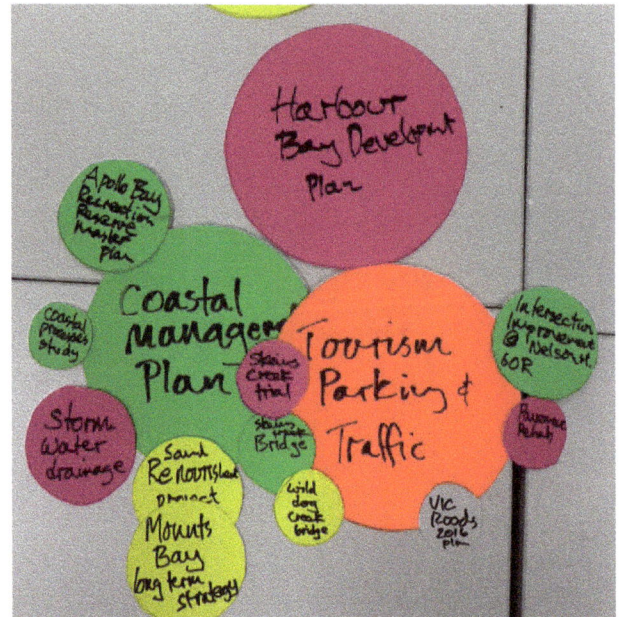

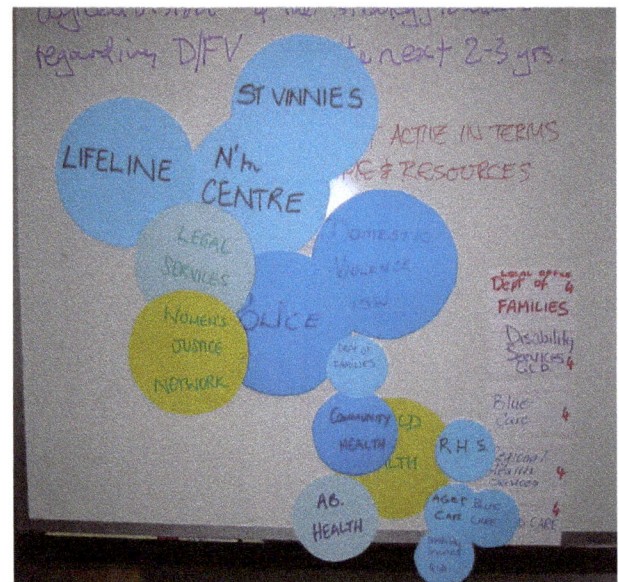

Figure 4.10 Two examples of Venn diagrams in use. The larger the roundel, the more power (or impact)

Process instructions:

Set out on the venue wall a relevant historic timeline. In some instances this might be years, in others months. Ask participants to work in pairs and write on individual cards the important, significant, crucial or catalytic events over the period. Allow participants about 10 minutes to do this, and then ask them to put the cards under the appropriate time spot on the wall. If participants are referring to a process or activity that extended over a period of time, ask them to write two cards, one for the beginning and another for the end.

If there are more than about 15 people in the group, there is likely to be quite a few duplications of the same event posted. Assign people to particular time zones to group the like cards together.

It there are fewer than six people in the group, it is sometimes useful to have individuals to put up cards as they think of them. This provides a useful springboard to others' recollections, and also honours those who are the holders of the story for their knowledge.

Once all cards are up on the wall, ask the team leader, knowledgeable person or a volunteer to read through the cards as a story from early times to the present day (Figure 4.11).

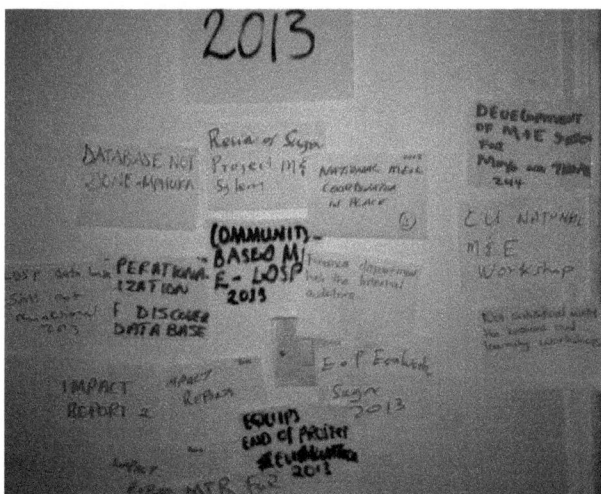

Figure 4.11 Detail of History Wall showing the variety of activities that happened in 2013

Combination techniques

Participatory analysis techniques are a great way to enable dialogue between participants.

Deliberation is more commonly understood to be the end of the process that pulls the conversation to a close.

Whilst not stringently adhering to the Diverge/ Groan Zone/Converge concept, there are a number of very useful workshop techniques that come close enough, techniques that help a group consider a topic and firm up their agreement.

Nominal group technique

(Group time 20–30 minutes)

Pairs think of solutions. In turn ask each pair to provide one solution. Encourage conversations if there are disagreements from others and write up agreed solutions.

Think Pair Share

(Group time 20–30 minutes)

Type: A small group dialogue and deliberation process

Theory:

1. Contrary to traditional brainstorming practice, subsequent analysis has shown that both better and more numerous answers to a question are generated by giving participants some time to think quietly and individually.

2. Sharing (Pair) with one other provides an opportunity for both individuals to find areas of commonality in a safe environment.

Sharing with the table group provides the diversity for some transcendental thinking to occur. The time spent by the table group working out how to find the top two best answers will in the best instances produce a deeper and more considered reply than that from any one individual.

Process instructions:

1. Give individuals time to answer the question in silence and individually (3 minutes).

2. Instruct participants to share their responses with their neighbour and

develop the top two answers (5 minutes). (Figure 4.12.)

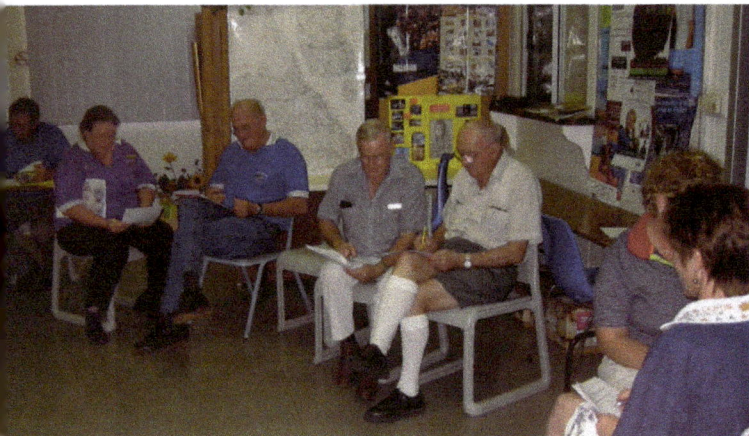

4.12 Discussing ideas in pairs, before joining together in fours.

3. Share with the table group and develop the top two answers (5 minutes).

Observations on use:

I find this a useful alternative to the more intense workshop techniques such as Card Storming or round robins. Generally, it seems to suit situations where personal experience is what is being looked for. An example is, 'What has been your greatest learning this fire season?' It allows individuals time to reflect on their own experience and then, talking with a colleague, they can find a common language for their shared experiences.

Silent Round Robin

(Group time 20–30 minutes)

Type: A small group dialogue and deliberation process.

A useful process for small teams.

Theory:

1. Many small groups are subject to group think, which is where individuals will modify their thinking dependent on potential ramifications outside of the group – that is, there might be problems

later if the boss's idea is not supported. This process helps divorce the ideas from the people in a small close group such as a team.

2. Seeing what others have written as an answer to a question often triggers new thoughts about the problem.

Process instructions:

1. Individuals to answer the question in silence and individually (3 minutes, write legibly!) (Figure 4.13).

4.13 Participants in table groups at a training workshop doing a Silent Round Robin.

2. Pass the sheet one person clockwise. Each person to read through their neighbour's ideas, and add new ideas (do not repeat what they wrote in the previous sheet).

3. Preferably repeat this (to get three people's ideas).

4. Repeat again and give a new instruction (the fourth person will now have three people's ideas on the sheet they have). This person is to select the top one or two ideas on the sheet in front of them.

5. Some of these will be similar but worded differently. The group can then find a collective wording for the idea.

Observations on use:

I always feel a bit self-conscious asking people to do this for real, that is, outside of a training situation. I'm not quite sure why because it produces good results in a short time, and in a far shorter time than an unstructured conversation.

Noisy Round Robin

(Preparation 10 minutes, Group time 20 – 30 minutes)

Type: A flexible small/large group process that combines both the dialogue and deliberation processes. It is remarkably flexible, with many different nuances and variations.

Theory:

Where there are large numbers, table groups working together provide a level of support to the individual but in turn can become a bit insulated. This process allows a large group to access what many are thinking. It achieves this by allowing small groups to discuss their thoughts on a topic and write them down on a sheet of flip-chart paper. Subsequently passing the sheet of paper to another group allows the second group to hear what the first group's thoughts are about the topic. By repeating the process three times, it allows three tables to see what others are also thinking about the topic.

Process instructions:

1. Instruct each table group to brainstorm their ideas to the question and write all on the sheet of flip-chart paper provided (7 minutes). (Figure 4.14)

2. Move the sheet one table clockwise. Each table to read through their neighbouring table's ideas and add new ideas. Do not repeat what was written on the previous sheet (5 minutes).

3. Preferably repeat this to get three table group's ideas (5 minutes).

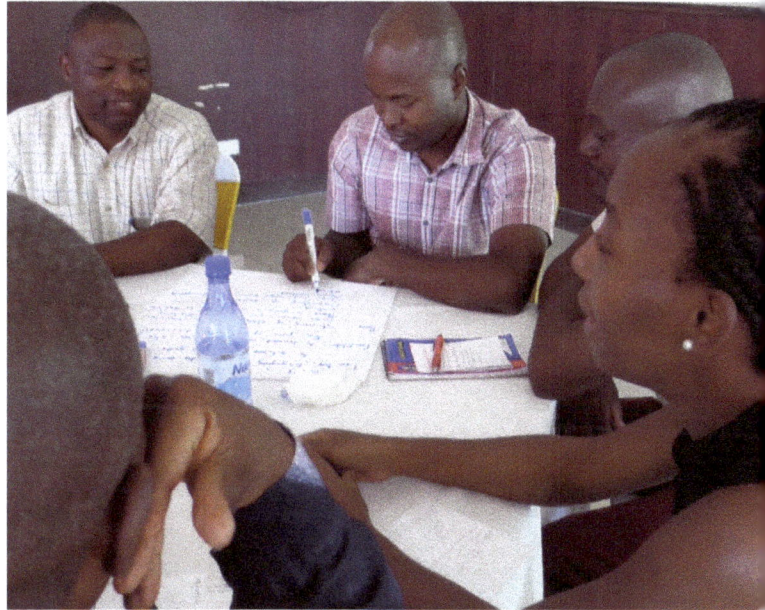

4.14 Table group participants contributing to a Noisy Round Robin.

4. Repeat again and give a new instruction (the fourth table will now have three table group's ideas on the sheet they have). This table group is to select the top one or two ideas on the sheet in front of them (5 minutes).

Observations on use:

This is probably one of the most frequently used workshop techniques I have in my toolbox. There is no limit to the number of topics I have asked groups to explore.

Variations:

There are two significant variations I have used. The first is where I have a number of different questions (usually one for each sheet). Thus, in the first round each table group is answering different questions. When they receive the first table's flip-chart sheet they are seeing a different question, including the earlier group's answers. I find it works well enough but suspect that the final products are not quite as well considered as when the whole group has been working on one question. However, when combined with the second variation, I think it works quite well.

The second variation is to pin the flip-chart paper up and move the people. I have read that people are more creative when standing up talking and more analytical when sitting down. Thus, by pinning up a number of questions and moving the groups around there is a greater emphasis on creativity and possibility for the group to record outside the box answers. For clarity I usually refer to this variation as the gallery process.

Card storm

(Preparation 10 minutes, Group time 30 – 40 minutes)

Type: A group sense-making process

Theory:

1. A characteristic of complex topics is that the same phenomena or observation are often described in different words. This is not the same as the same event being interpreted differently, just described differently.

2. By working together on what each person sees and describes separately, individuals can gain a greater understanding of the topic through sharing their own perspectives with the group and seeking a common understanding.

3. It is a useful technique to achieve Grounded Theory in practice.

Process instructions:

1. Have participants work in pairs to brainstorm onto A6 cards or sheets of paper every answer they have to the focus question (7 minutes).

2. Ask each pair to hand up their card with the most relevant (or important) answer (5 minutes).

3. Ask the whole group if there are any cards saying the same thing. Place those cards together.

4. Ask pairs to pass up their next important card, then their most way-out card, followed by any cards that fit any group. Between each of these, keep asking for cards to be grouped.

5. Once all the cards have been passed up, the probability is that there will be between 4–10 groups.

6. Starting with one group of cards, ask participants for the heading that would describe the group. This process is most important, as it forces participants into new and emergent thinking. (Figure 4.15)

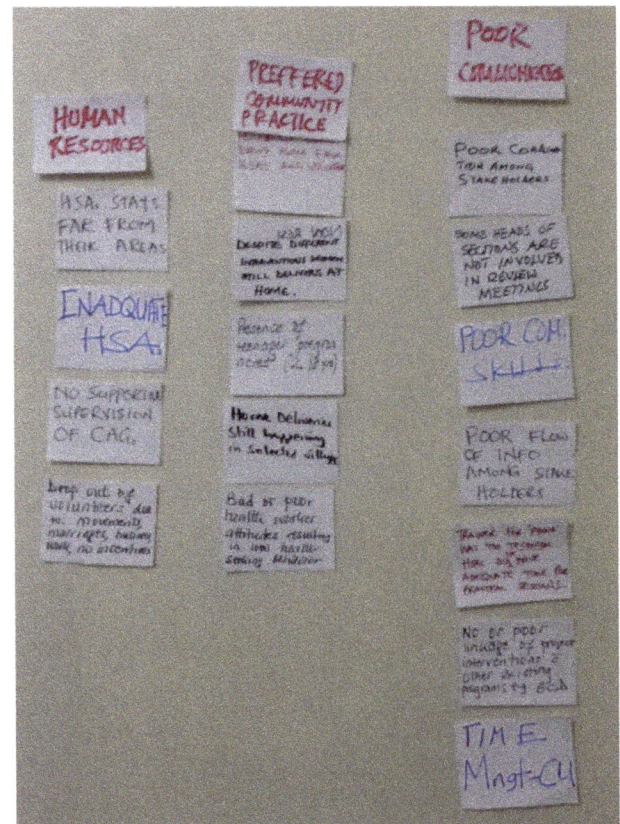

4.15 Cards expressing similar ideas grouped and named.

Observations on use:

This is a highly flexible and useful workshop process. However, its most useful underlying benefit is also its weakness. Coming up with the names for each group of cards is hard work. I recall using the process for every part of a small workshop, and it was just simply too demanding. I now ration its use to once a day, always when I have decided which is the most critical component for deep thinking.

More recently I have found a slightly faster and less intense variation, which is to ask all cards to be placed on a table, and participants to stand around the table and group them (silently). Once grouped, and making sure that all cards sit within one of the groups, I will ask for the headers.

Action planning

Action plan presentations

(Preparation 10 minutes, Group time 20–30 minutes)

Type: A method that promotes individual learning as part of the Action Learning cycle.

Theory:

1. The Action Research cycle is also known as Action Learning. Both require something to be carried out to reflect and learn from.
2. Creating a plan is a statement of intent from which the individual can learn.
3. Being a supportive colleague is more helpful than being a critical friend.
4. Describing an intended course of action helps refine the proposal and thinking.

Process instructions:

1. Have participants develop their own plan of action, either as individuals or in pairs or groups of 3. Allow 20 minutes. (Any more and people lose concentration.)
2. Ensure that participants describe their plan to their peers (in pairs or small groups). Have the one who is most vested in the project to stay with their plan. Ask all others to visit another project proposal. Allow about 7–10 minutes per presentation round. Allow a

minimum of two rounds, and a maximum of three. In two rounds the project driver or owner has the chance to explain their project to others, and also see another's plan (Figure 4.16).

Figure 4.16 Presenting the proposal to peers. Having to articulate an idea helps clarify one's own understanding.

3. After presenting, participants have the opportunity to return to their group, or have time as an individual to modify their proposal

Observations on use:

I have found this consistently beneficial in situations where a variety of participants are wanting to develop their own action plans. This can be for any topic relevant to the focus of the workshop. Initially I thought it would be important that everybody has a chance to develop their own plan, but in practice this has not proved to be the case. Most times I find that there are a few that want to develop a plan for their project (or subproject) and others are quite happy to be supporters.

Gantt Charts

(Group time 40–60 minutes)

Helping a group to plan their project

Theory:

Once a group has identified a SMART (Specific, Measurable and Actionable in Real Time) product to create, it is then helpful for them to develop a Gantt chart that sets out the steps required to achieve the finished product.

Process instructions:

Pin up a series of timecards chronologically on a wall that reflect a realistic time scale for the project.

Sometimes a group develops a number of products they need to achieve. If this is the case, write cards for each and fix these down the side of the calendar.

Ask each sub-project (or milestone) group to determine what date they will achieve that milestone, or complete the sub-project and place a card with that name at the appropriate date.

Ask each group to complete at least two cards identifying what/who/when actions that need to be done to achieve that sub-project or milestone. Once all are on the wall, a conversation can be had with the whole team to see if the plan is realistic. (Figure 4.17)

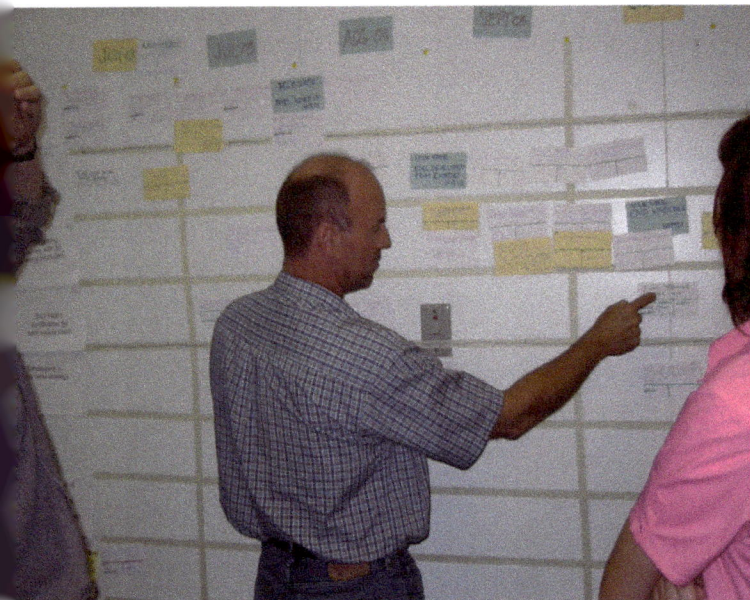

Figure 4.17 Action Planning for a large project with dates across the top and different milestones down the left-hand side.

Asynchronous large-scale processes

The fundamentals of workshop design processes can also be translated into asynchronous events. This is where not everyone is in the room at the same time. The same conceptual frameworks are utilised, but the difference is that there might be a number of events in each of the three Diverge/Converge parts of a process. Enabling people to hear what others have already said might require whole events in their own right.

In the Diverge part of a large-scale event, useful tools are:

1. Semi-structured interviews
2. Open House
3. Listening Post

In the groan zone or dialogue part of the process, useful tools are:

4. Facilitated workshops generally
5. World Cafe
6. Open Space Technology (OST)
7. Study circles

In the Converge or Deliberation part of the process:

1. Ranking processes generally
2. Participatory Budgeting.

Kitchen Table Discussions (KTDs)

Description: A relaxed informal setting between a facilitator and a small group of people with a common interest. The title of this community engagement technique does not have to be taken literally, though it implies a certain informality that is an essential element.

The venue does not have to be a kitchen table; it might well be a cafe or pub or similar venue.

The purpose of the technique is to both hear others' views, and also hear where there are differences between the individuals in the group.

Benefits: It is especially useful when there is a topic that needs further exploration, both at the beginning and during a process. This technique lends itself to cohesive social groups, such as members of a club, etc.

It is also especially good for people to learn about the differences between one another, without it being made an obvious objective.

Participants are only required to commit themselves to one meeting, though they may volunteer to meet again (Figure 4.18).

Figure 4.18 Facilitated Kitchen Table Discussions are a great way for small groups to learn from each other.

Limitations: When part of a community-wide engagement process, it is a dialogue tool rather than a deliberation (decision-making) tool.

Other considerations: There are various methods of getting a group together. It is often possible to find hosts who will invite a few others to attend a discussion – especially if you promise to provide the cakes and refreshments.

An approach is to ask a significant contact if they would like to ask some of their friends to meet with you. This way there is less likelihood of conflict than if you made the invitations to individuals who do not know each other.

Semi-Structured Interviews (SSIs)

Sometimes called key-stakeholder or 'one-on-one' interviews.

Description: A 'one-on-one'interview technique that allows the interviewee space to elaborate on a set of broad, open, questions. Useful at the beginning of a project.

Benefits: Provides the interviewer the chance to get to meet and hear the person being interviewed. It provides the interviewee the potential of meeting a key person in the project.

Weaknesses: Expertise in qualitative analysis is required to make best use of the findings. It is generally not possible to interview all community members, and it can be resource-intensive.

Skills: A number of skills are required to carry out semi-structured interviews successfully.

1. The first is preparing the questions. These need to be 'open-ended' questions, designed to provide a context for the interviewee to respond and elaborate on.

2. A skilled interviewer. The interviewers need not have developed the questions, but they need to be good listeners and have sufficient understanding of the project to know when and how to allow the conversation to flow.

Other considerations:

1. It is a resource-costly engagement technique. It is often best used with carefully targeted individuals, such as the politically powerful, or those with specialist knowledge in the project topic.

2. It is best if the interviewer makes the effort to meet the interviewee on his or her own turf. It further demonstrates that you value their time, and are prepared to make the effort to see them.

This technique is most useful for people with power in the community, or who are technical experts in the topic.

Theory:

In every group decision-making process, it is important to understand how people exert power, and what those with power over others expect. In large-scale engagement processes it is those with institutional power and specialist information who like to feel that they are being given special treatment.

Process instructions:

Make an appointment to meet at a convenient place for the interviewee. Usually that is at their home or office.

Ask for 20 minutes of their time, but allow an hour yourself. That means that if on the day of the interview they want to keep talking past the 20 minutes, you are not the one rushing out the door.

Develop about 3–5 focus questions. I like to base these on the ORID framework, often using a variation of:

1. How long have you lived here? (The purpose of the question is more to help break the ice than to discover the answer.)

2. What have been some of the highlights?

3. What about challenges?

4. Thinking about the future, if everything went really well, what would you see, feel, hear in the community?

Make notes. Write up a synopsis and send it back to the interviewee asking for corrections to anything you might have misunderstood.

Observations on use:

I find this technique is really appreciated. It helps build relationships and trust. I have heard that some practitioners like to use a tape recorder, but I find it too difficult subsequently to provide a useful synopsis of the meeting.

I often extract comments and statements later (and, importantly, de-identify them) for use in more public feedback sessions.

Open House

The Open House or drop-in event is one of the most useful, versatile and adaptable large-scale event techniques. The technique can be used successfully at every point of the Diverge/ Converge model.

Theory:

Today's communities are diverse. Individuals within a common geographic area have different worldviews, and often different everyday commitments. The community is not a homogeneous body. The inhabitants of a village 200 years ago might have had many shared life experiences, common worldview and vision. Today this would be rare.

In earlier times a community meeting could be organised with a time that would suit almost everyone, with an agenda that would suit all, and speakers from the floor who would genuinely reflect the views of the many. Today, none of this is true.

The Open House concept allows for:

1. Community members to visit at a time that suits them.

2. A safe environment in which to express one's own views.

Figure 4.19 Open House events are highly flexible.

3. Opportunities to gain the information that is relevant to oneself.

4. Opportunities to hear what other participants' views are (Figure 4.19).

Process instructions:

Work with the project manager to clearly identify what the Negotiables and Not Negotiables are at the time.

Develop a series of posters that articulates the history and current state of the project. Use plain language, and no more than 200 words per poster. Illustrate each poster with useful drawings or diagrams. Redraw technical drawings so that the elements that need to be illustrated stand alone. (Most technical drawings contain large amounts of information.)

Talk with key gatekeeper members of the target community about times and venue for the event. Be conscious of the potential for venues to be the domain of a particular stakeholder group.

Decide on and advertise a variety of time slots.

Observations on use:

1. Brief and train staff on how to listen.

2. Have a variety of project staff and technical consultants available at all times.

3. Make sure the hours suit the target audience.

4. Be ready an hour before opening time. Someone always turns up early.

5. Have someone to greet people personally at the door.

6. Collect last thoughts as participants leave.

7. Only collect the information you need regarding the participants; numbers and postcodes is usually sufficient.

8. Provide a wide variety of ways for people to interact with the content.

9. Collate the information and feed back what was heard ASAP after the event.

10. Have the displays set up as multi-space to inhibit the take-over by a passionate few.

Limitations: I have found a limitation of a general public Open House event is that they tend to attract the older and more educated members of the community. Linking them with Listening Posts helps (at a school, outside the mosque etc.), or just recognizing this and using other engagement methods relevant for different cohorts.

Listening Post (LP)

Listening posts are similar but different to Open Houses. Both comprise supported interactive displays. The big difference between the two is that Open Houses are usually in a location where participants have to go, whilst a listening post is more like a pop-up where people are already (Figure 4.20).

4.20 Listening Posts are set up where those with an interest in the topic are already. A literal interpretation of meeting people where they're at.

Theory

As with Open House, the theory is that today's communities are diverse and have diverse values. Not everyone is willing or able to get to an Open House event, but might well contribute whilst at the market or in the shopping strip.

Process instructions:

1. Prepare a small amount of information material.

2. Check the permit regulations for your intended spot.

3. Design to accommodate all weathers.

4. Brief and train staff on how to listen and write at the same time.

5. Have a variety of ways for participants to record their input.

Have easels with flip-charts to record people's input. In some instances having a dedicated listener and associated scribe is worthwhile.

If it is a complex topic with many different areas of issues and concerns, consider having a string of listening posts at the one event, each focusing on different topics such as: parking; playgrounds; the foreshore; crime prevention.

Observations on use:

There is quite a lot of crossover between an Open House and a Listening Post. Of most importance is to have a short opener to attract people, together with a focus question. It is not sufficient to stand mutely behind a table of brochures.

Open Space Technology (OST)

Invented in the 1980s by Harrison Owen, an organisational consultant and conference organiser, this technique is extremely useful where there is a complex situation involving a large number of people with no clear direction.

Theory:

The origin of the process is supposedly based on an observation by Harrison Owen that when people attend a conference, what they find the most exciting and important happens in the breaks. A more nuanced theory is that complex problems exist in a complex system, and OST responds appropriately to this. When the problem has no single solution, and there are many actors involved, starting with those that have passion to drive change is a reasonable place to start.

Open Space Technology (OST) is a method for organising and running a meeting or multi-day conference, where participants have been invited in order to focus on a specific, important task or purpose. OST is a participant-driven process whose agenda is created by people attending. At the end of each OST meeting, a document is created summarising the work of the group. The OST method is based upon work, beginning in the 1980s, by Harrison Owen. It was one of the top ten organisation development tools cited between 2004 and 2013.[1]

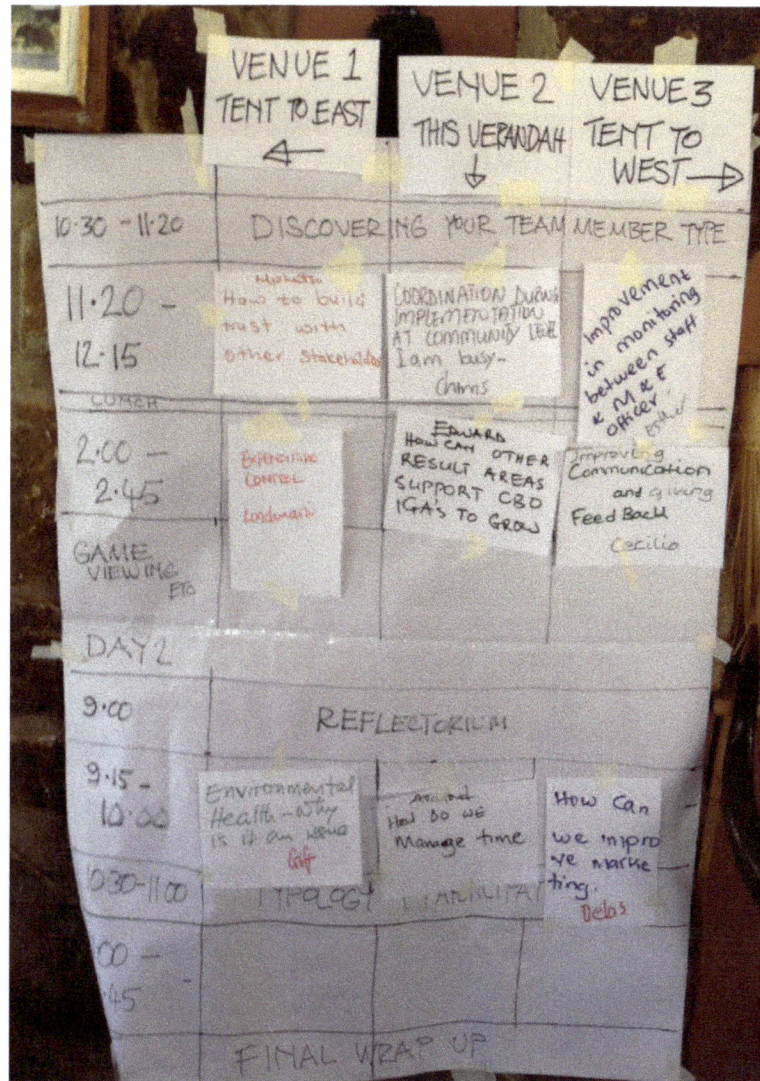

Figure 4.21 The critical part of Open Space Technology is that the agenda is developed at the beginning of the session by the participants. The session proposer is responsible for running the session.

the strength of the process is allowing the agenda to be set by the participants. The bit more is what happens after the event. My current view is that there has to be recognition of how OST is essentially a brainstorming and early dialogue process, and that the various groups that form during the event need additional support afterwards to progress ideas further.

Observations on use:

I have only run a true OST workshop three times, once in outback Queensland, and twice in Malawi (Figure 4.21). All three worked all right, but all seemed to need a bit more. On reflection,

In terms of the fundamentals of the process, I have often used the concept at the beginning of smaller workshops/meetings when there are fewer than about ten participants. In this instance I will first run a short session to elicit the topics people want to talk about, and then allocate the items in terms of time, not space: each topic has equal time. This might be only 10 minutes, but it means a conversation has been held about it and from there it can be organised for people to take the topic further outside of the meeting.

World Cafe

World Cafe is the second of pre-designed workshop techniques that can work either as a stand-alone workshop process, or be a component of a wider process. Designed by Juanita Brown and David Isaacs, this technique is a very versatile and useful technique to help workshop participants explore different topics.

A singular difference between World Cafe and OST is the determination of the topics for discussion. If, for whatever reason, the organisers have already determined what the topics for discussion should be then World Cafe is the preferable technique.

Theory:

When people meet in small groups, in a congenial environment and considering the questions that matter to them, they individually and collectively learn (Figure 4.22).

Figure 4.22 World Cafe technique is highly versatile, and always goes better with appropriate sustenance.

Process instructions:

More precise instructions are available on: http://www.theworldcafe.com/key-concepts-resources/world-cafe-method/.

The organisers have to develop a number of focus questions that will be of interest to the group. The precise number is flexible, conditioned by the number of people, the time available, and how much you want them to be involved in every question.

Organise the tables in cabaret style with about 6 –8 chairs per table. This is where the calculation needs to be done on the total number of questions. However, more rounds can be added enabling people to visit and participate in more than three conversations.

Plan for about 20 minutes per round, and about three rounds. Allow additional time for a synopsis from each table at the end of the session.

A critical part of the World Cafe process is to have cafe hosts or conveyors of meaning at each table. These people stay at their table and summarise the conversation there.

Either determine who these might be beforehand, or it can be decided through asking for volunteers on the day.

On the day, simply outline the process and keep people on time.

Observations on use:

I often use the World Cafe format in workshops. My preference is to have cafe hosts (or table facilitators) organised beforehand. This is primarily because most participants at an event want to move around and be part of more than one conversation.

My ideal times are to allow a full 20 minutes for each round, perhaps varying it a little depending on whether there is tea and coffee provided. I find when working with community groups it really helps to have the organisers act as waiters;

it demonstrates that we value the participants' time talking.

About half-way through the last round I always interrupt the conversations to ask participants to help the cafe host develop a two-minute synopsis of the table conversations. This is the critical part, and always needs to be part of the process.

Bi-focals

Commissioned by the Department of Sustainability & Environment Victoria, this process was designed to enable groups with different ideas about a topic to hear each other and come to an agreed way forward. The following is the original format, though I have often used cut-down versions as part of other workshops. The important part is that the groups each have a turn to talk within themselves whilst the others listen. It is not a debate.

Through listening to each other they are then more able to jointly develop a way forward that will meet both their requirements.

Preparation:

Invite between five to eight members of each group to attend a workshop to help resolve problems that you see are occurring. Explain that this will be a workshop. Invite exactly the same number (+/-1) from each group for a 10:30 am start.

Hire a suitable neutral venue. Arrange morning tea (10.30 am) and lunch (12.30 pm) for the total number of attendees. Arrange two seating formations.

1. Two circles of chairs, an inner circle and an outer circle, each circle matching the size of one group.

2. As many chairs as participants around a square or round dining table (not a rectangular or narrow table).

Process instructions:

1. It is best to have about eight people from each group. Equal numbers to ensure that one group does not feel outnumbered by the other, and about eight because that results in sixteen

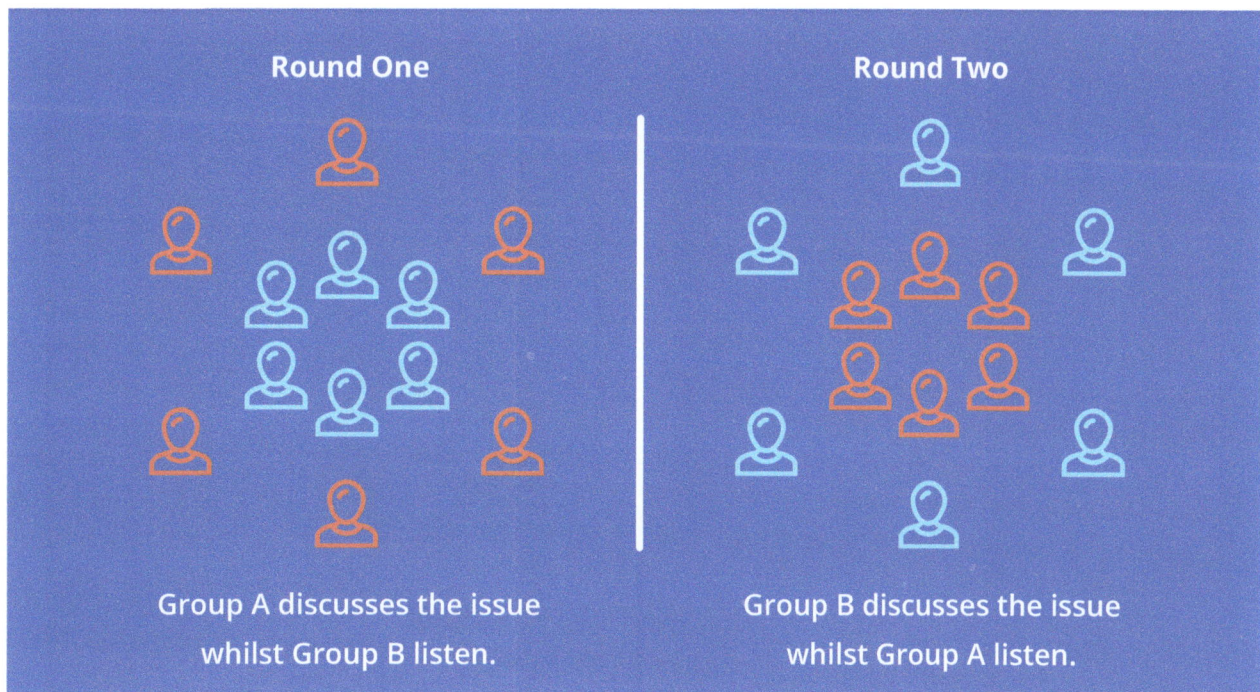

Round One

Round Two

Group A discusses the issue
whilst Group B listen.

Group B discusses the issue
whilst Group A listen.

Figure 4.23 The 'Bi-focal' process is a structured way for two different groups with a different frame on a situation able to hear each other, and subsequently look for a transcendental solution.

total. More would be difficult to manage; fewer, and the richness of the conversations is diminished (Figure 4.23).

2. The timing is important, with NO BREAK between Group A and Group B listening.

3. Welcome and outline of session 10 minutes.

4. Group A: The individuals in this group talk to each other about the situation from their perspective (45 minutes). The facilitator keeps the conversation within the group, not between the groups.

5. Group B: Repeat with Group B talking (45 minutes).

6. Joint session: over lunch where participants are encouraged to look for a way forward 45 minutes

7. A number of skills are required. A community engagement practitioner will need to have made the effort to build relationships between the groups with different values beforehand. Both groups will then be expecting a clean event that will not prove to be adversarial. On the day, a key skill is for the facilitator is to politely but firmly ensure that the listening group do not talk amongst themselves, interrupt, or are in any way disrespectful of the talking group.

Study Circles

Used extensively in Scandinavian countries, study circles provide small groups of community members the opportunity to consider a balance of views, opinions and information on complex topics in a structured process (Figure 4.24).

A typical process is:

1. The responsible authority prepares relevant background material including all views on the topic.

Fig 4.24 Study Circles are similar to Kitchen Table Discussions, though are usually more structured in their organisation. Everyday Democracy started out as the Study Circles Resource Center, and provides many resources to those wanting to start or participate in a Study Circles process. (See www.everyday-democracy.org)

2. Study circle facilitators are trained

3. Community members are invited to form groups of approximately 10–15 to meet for a set number of meetings, for instance, four.

4. Study group facilitators assist members to discuss the material, and develop recommendations.

Participatory Budgeting

Participatory Budgeting (PB) is a formalised methodology to describe a process in which groups of people develop ideas and then determine from a set budget which will get funded from the funds available. It was initially developed in both India and Brazil and is now being used in diverse locations including New York. It has support from the World Bank and has a good track record for empowering individuals and groups. It is though for these very reasons not as popular amongst those with power to allocate funds within traditional structures and processes.

Within the Australian context a common process is for committees to advertise for grant applications and then make awards based on stated criteria. Participatory budgeting is where those that make applications are also the ones making the decisions. There are numerous ways in which this can be organised, though an accepted practice is:

1. Community members identify spending priorities and select budget delegates;

2. Budget delegates develop specific spending proposals, with help from experts;

3. Community members vote on which proposals to fund;

4. The city or institution implements the top proposals.

However there are many other options, including simple versions such as where delegates are all given an equal number of sticker dots that together total the budget available.

Summary

I have found these tools and techniques useful and robust. They fit within the idea of design or decision-making being a series of Diverge/Converge activities, that in turn also correspond to the iterative nature of development as described in the Action Research cycle. Whilst I have grouped these tools and techniques into six key areas, in practice I'm quite likely to use one in a manner or situation outside of the context written.

Some examples of how I've organised these concepts and techniques follow.

CHAPTER 5

Theory in use: Bringing the ideas to life

When designing decision-making workshops and processes I have found many analogies to the world of architecture and the built environment. The most significant is the infinite variety of ways to fulfil a brief. Getting a coherent brief is, in itself, an Action Research process with many discussions with and suggestions from the project owner to develop the running sheet – a running sheet being simply the plan for a participatory workshop or process.

When I collect the brief my intention is to use the information provided to create a linear series of techniques which, together with the questions to be asked, will allow participants the space for useful conversations with each other. In terms of design process, just as I found it quicker and easier to work directly with the client when designing a house, I have found this to be also true when designing workshops. My own preference now is to work directly with the project owner and develop the workshop design together in real time. This has not always been the case. I remember in the early days of designing workshops, I would spend weeks going backwards and forwards with the client refining what was required and how to fulfil it.

There are three major parameters that guide my approach to a workshop plan. Two of these are purely pragmatic: the time available and the number of participants. The third is based on the project owner's perception of a successful workshop. Sometimes this is clear from the start, often not. There are other dynamics affecting which technique to use at any given time, but these are secondary. Examples are how well participants know each other, the time available, the time slot in the program. But at a fundamental level it is these three elements that provide the sturdiest anchors to guide the design approach.

This is not to say that all workshops are designed in one short sitting. Many do require multiple meetings with the project owner. In some ways I think that within the context of achieving good outcomes to Wicked problems, there is a further analogy between designing workshops and designing buildings. Both are self-contained products that exist in space and time. Both can be mundane and uninteresting to be in or, conversely, exciting and inspirational.

My own goal or desired outcome for every workshop is that by the end everybody will feel that they have found every minute of their time both useful and enjoyable.

With only two clear exceptions, (the LogFrame sequence and the stakeholder engagement planning sequence) every workshop I design is unique. Even then, I will often tailor the details. The parameters are too wide for a cookie-cutter approach.

Whilst no two workshops are the same, I have developed a personal vocabulary that gives good service.

Some of the design elements are:

1. The context

2. The underlying emphasis (outcome/output)

3. The number of people involved (1/20/50 etc.)

4. The time available (hours/days)

5. Where the desired resolution fits on the Diverge/Converge scale (part/full)

6. The nature of the participants (similar values/random/diverse)

7. Where the current situation fits on the Action Learning cycle (scope/plan/reflect)

8. What success would look like if the workshop/product/decision or engagement process was fantastic.

Spending time on activities that just help people get to know each other at a personal level is often hard to argue for with time-poor clients, but is always worth the time spent. Sometimes known as icebreakers, these activities are equally valuable even for workshops where the participants have met before, or even worked together before. The difference might be around the level of disclosure that the questions elicit, or the number of people they are expected to share their thoughts and beliefs with.

Of particular concern is the need to ameliorate power, or to use practices that enables the less powerful opportunities to express their worldviews and ideas. The naturally more confident will always make their views and ideas known.

Discussion groups

My preferred strategy is to design workshops based on small group discussions. I vary how they might occur, from sitting at small tables, talking in pairs, developing ideas whilst standing

in triads. I will also mix the groups up to ensure lots of variety in who talks with whom.

At a structural level, I have become aware that an overlay of the Action Learning model and Diverge/Converge concept provides a seemingly infinite variety of options. I am reminded of an architectural analogy in how Le Corbusier had two sequences of ratios based on the Golden Rectangle and Fibonacci scales – the Modulor. It provided him a limited palette that, used in combination, provided structure to a (possibly) infinite variety of situations. When I reflect on how I approach designing a workshop, I can now see that most designs are from playing with these two concepts to satisfy the brief. Each of the concepts has its own characteristics, both useful and limiting.

There are various interpretations or descriptions of the Action Learning/Design cycle, but I have found Figure 5.1 works for me. I use this version of the concept in two significant ways. The first is to plan and develop the workshop running sheet, the second as a structure to a running

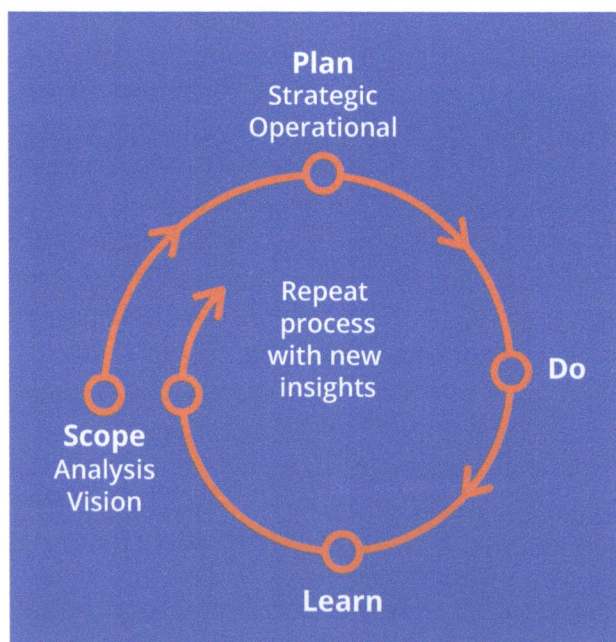

Figure 5.1 The Design or Action Learning model. Scoping the current reality needs to be an articulation of the desired goal, as well as an analysis of the current reality. The word plan encompasses two different concepts. 1) Answering the question why? 2) Answering the question how?

sheet itself. This is not always the case, but an approach I often use.

When collecting the brief, I will ask 'What would success look like, if this workshop is really successful?' The answer is always useful. I will also ask early in the discussion functional questions such as:

1. How many people?
2. How long?
3. When? Where?

The project owner will then offer a wide description of why they want this particular workshop. The challenge is to tease out the key points, and identify what questions need to be answered by the group. On occasions this is not easy. I recall a number of conversations where I have listened to what is required, and I have then responded, 'So, the question we should be asking the group is...', followed by more dialogue and a different story emerging, which in turn results in me devising a completely different question. On one memorable occasion, I still don't think we landed with the best questions, possibly because the topic was to ask the participants to identify specific indicators to climate change when the connections between the indicators and climate change were highly variable and complex.

I have had many conversations with colleagues about which should come first, analysis or vision? I am now firmly of the opinion it doesn't matter. What is more likely is the need for a backward/forward process between the two. Or, alternatively, it depends on some other factor, such as how well people know each other, either before or after lunch.

In practice, I often find that a work group has a defined goal or outcome already set out for them. In these cases it's just a matter of reminding everyone of the situation.

In other instances there is no clearly articulated common goal for the group. There will be a

general goal stated by the one giving the brief, which is a good start for the design of the the workshop. However, there might be a need for the whole group to develop a collective vision to work towards.

Unless the focus of the workshop is specifically to obtain a common vision, or mission statement (which is very rarely asked for), I won't expect participants to spend hours refining a common vision. A few dot points is generally sufficient for a group to work towards.

Scoping

I use the word scoping to describe what is often referred to as PAR. Essentially I design a variety of exercises based around mapping, ranking and scoring activities. The intention is to help the group share their understanding of the current reality. In the process, there are often areas of difference as well as areas of commonality. Usually, all that is needed is an understanding that there is difference, rather than any need to come to a common agreement. Many of the same techniques can be used in the scoping part of the AR cycle, as the reflection part. This is natural because the end of one cycle is generally the beginning of another. In practice, it is usually the brief that dictates whether the weight or emphasis for a workshop is on reflection (what happened) or analysis (what is happening).

Just as there are similarities and blurring of distinctions between whether the purpose is analysis or reflection, ranking and scoring techniques are equally transferable.

When Participatory Analysis techniques were first invented for the Rapid Rural Assessment program, asking villagers to draw their environment in the dirt using sticks and stones provided everyone with various insights into how the village worked. I often use a variation of this using sticker dots on photocopied maps (Figure 5.2). Questions can be quite simple, such as: 'Where do you live?' or more reflective: 'Place

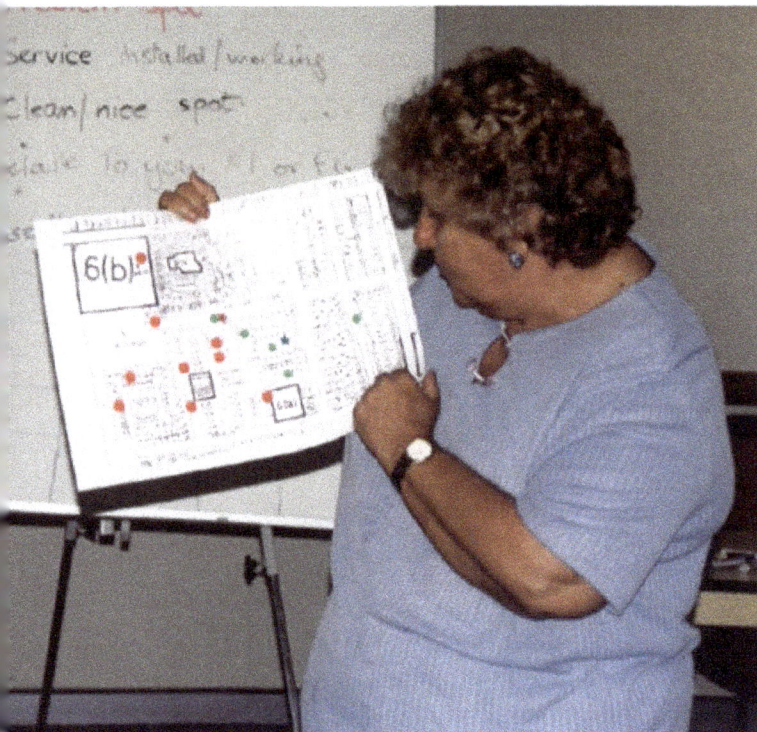

Figure 5.2 A workshop participant explaining her view of the neighbourhood.

red sticker dots on the areas where you don't feel so safe, or don't like, and green ones on the areas you feel comfortable in.' Again, it is in the interpretation and discussion that people become more aware of where their synergies and differences lie.

The intention behind all these processes is to create a *safe place* for people to talk and listen. A wide variety of opportunities will help ensure more than just a small group are involved in the process.

Planning

The next step in the Action Learning/Design cycle is planning, both strategic and operational.

Whilst I have continually found the sequence developed by the Institute of Cultural Affairs as part of their Technology of Participation (ToP) process possibly the most robust way for a group to develop a strategic plan, I never seem to have the time available as demanded by ToP.

Thus my workshop designs often comprise ways to speed the process up. One way to achieve this is to treat each question as its own mini Diverge/Converge problem using any one of the combination techniques. Depending on the situation, as each question brings a number of possibilities upon which to base the next part of the process, I might use some form of ranking question or process to help clarify the next step. Which technique I use depends on the particular situation.

Once participants have identified some outputs to undertake, I will have them rank those that they think are the most easy/hard, and more or less effective (Figure 5.3).

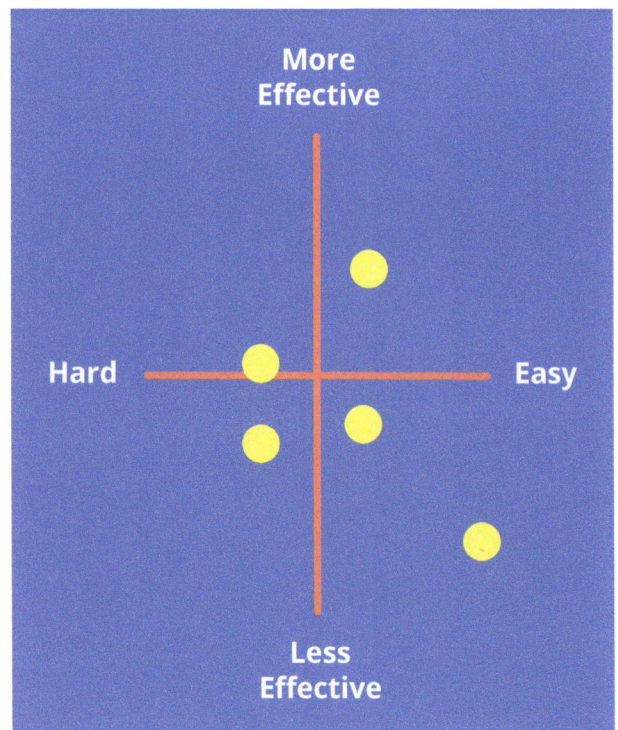

Figure 5.3 By asking participants to first rank their solutions/ outputs according to effectiveness, followed by how difficult to implement them helps them understand their solutions better.

This piece of analysis will help them understand the scope of the tasks ahead a little more, but the critical part is to find a driver. It is passion that changes the world, and just because a certain course or action is logical or makes sense doesn't mean it will be taken. Thus once the group has identified the possible outputs, I will seek out who has the passion and ask who will be the driver for any proposed project. The intention is that the driver will engage the others and be the project manager. It does not mean that the driver will do all the work. If there is no-one willing to take on this role, that's the way it is. It means it will not proceed. When working with teams that comprise paid staff, I am finding that there is a greater understanding within those institutions that such roles need funding and time, with the work often being delegated to specific teams.

I find the operational planning part of planning is often best achieved through using the wall-size version of a Gantt Chart as described in Chapter 4 (Figure 5.4).

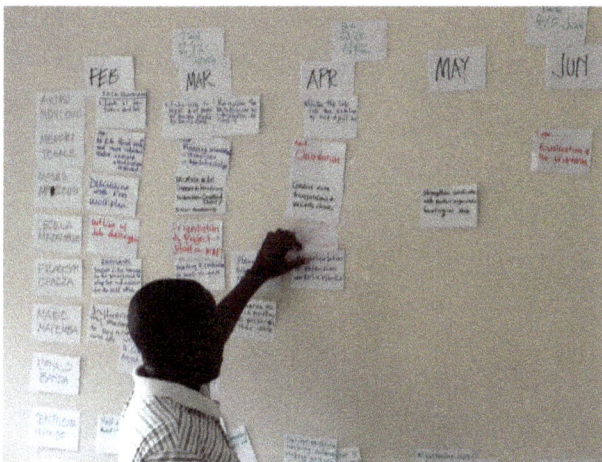

Figure 5.4 Action planning on the wall.

Diverge/Converge

As discussed previously, it is the interrelation of the Action Learning and the Diverge/Converge concepts that form the basis of almost every workshop I design.

The three components of diverge/groan zone/converge well reflect my own experience of designing buildings. At the start is a cacophony of ideas and criteria and values and inspiration and possibilities, working towards a solution that invariably transitions into a stage of despair and frustration. To get through this stage into

creating something meaningful and fit for purpose requires focus and commitment, combined with openness and willingness to change.

Diverge

The Diverge section of any kind of engagement process is the easiest to understand. The principle is for the participants to hear all the voices on a particular topic. I don't think it is necessary for the facilitator to do so.

An early and well-known example of hearing all the voices is brainstorming. The classic image is a facilitator standing at the front of a room with a flip-chart, calling for participants to shout out their ideas. I have done this occasionally, and in some particular instances it works, most usually for two or three participants. There are also other reasons why the process is deficient.

The first is group think. Group think is where somebody will modify their contribution because of their relationship with another outside of the workshop. This is often because there is a power difference external to the workshop (boss, neighbour etc) or simply because of the desire to be seen as one of the gang.

In a similar vein, many are simply shy and reluctant to express views in front of a large group of others that they don't know for fear of how they might be perceived as an individual. Additionally there are significant drawbacks, such as:

1. The speed of collecting ideas is restricted to how fast the facilitator can write.

2. It is difficult to manage both where the ideas are coming from as well as to write them down, so usually it is the confident and loud people that get their ideas up.

3. The conversation rarely stays on the task of brainstorming, and usually

results in all kinds of digressions and observations. There are ample opportunities for participants to digress and discuss an idea, especially when the suggestion to do so comes from the powerful person in the group. I specifically remember one senior public servant who had an uncanny knack of disrupting any kind of brainstorm process with requests to 'let's just unpack that a little'.

If I do use this method to hear all the voices, I now either modify this method or restrict it to specific uses.

When there are only two or three participants, I sit at the table with them with a large sheet of paper and markers. I allow some digressions, and ask for clarity on things I don't understand, but I am focused on getting ideas from them all. This results in a messy product but sets out the various thoughts at the table for all to see. Another situation is where, for some reason, hearing all the voices is not really the intention of the exercise.

Recently I wanted a group of about 50 people who did not know each other to both understand the parameters of a grant program they were interested in and to get to know each other a little better. Two key criteria for successful applications in the program was for groups to work collaboratively and create innovative solutions. I had arranged the venue in cafe seating format with between four and eight participants on each table. After a brief overview of the grants program and a Q&A session, I started the process by asking participants to discuss with those at their table what they thought the words *innovation* and *collaboration* meant. After 10 minutes of table group discussion I called for examples of what innovation meant. If the answer was long, I would paraphrase it. In this instance I had scribes work side by side taking turns to write up the suggestions. After about 5 minutes we had a broad range of answers and I called a

halt. I then repeated the process for what *collaboration* meant to the group.

In this instance the 'shout it out' brainstorm approach was appropriate because the intention was as much to get the participants talking with each other to start building relationships as it was to illustrate the wide variety of meanings associated with each of those words. There was no need to hear every person's views on the meaning of these two words.

In the early days of working in this field I had to organise three sessions for an external facilitator to work with public housing residents. At the last session, when a lady announced that the big issues for the estate were drugs and alcohol, it did not go down well when the facilitator retorted 'Oh, we know that already'. It is important that each person's perspective is listened to and their views taken seriously. The aim is more than just data collection; for an effective process, it is engagement and relationship building. To build trust requires treating people seriously.

The intention is to get out all the ideas into the public realm, and enable people to express their ridiculous ideas without being ridiculed. To achieve this I have had most success by providing ways for ideas to be separated from the people that generate them at every step of the way. It helps allow people to discuss the ideas, not burdened by preconceptions of whose idea it is.

Thus, whether it is a small group working at the same time (especially if there is distinct power differences amongst the participants) or a large asynchronous group process, I have consistently found using ways that separate the individuals from the opinions or ideas expressed to be the most fruitful. And the most reliable method is to provide a mechanism for the idea or opinion to be written down. Once written down, the idea is on its own. Once everyone feels heard by seeing their idea written, they are then more likely to actively engage in dialogue.

In practice I have found that successfully working with a group is a sequence of one Diverge/Converge activity after another. For small workshop situations I use a mixture of my favourite techniques which achieve the whole Diverge/Converge process in one. These are Noisy Round Robin, Silent Round Robin, Card Storming, Think/Pair/Share, and Gallery. There are benefits of each, though often my rationale for using one rather than another is to maintain variety over the course of a workshop.

Sequential Diverge/Converge

In practice, I have found the Noisy Round Robin process extremely robust in quickly providing individuals in a group the opportunity to reach the beginnings of consensus. The process is for small groups to brainstorm their solutions to a problem, then see others' solutions, and finally to pick out the best from all three rounds. I am consistently impressed with the quality of the answers provided. In a relatively short period of time, good-quality thinking has identified key responses to a complex problem. The following step is dependent on the situation, but a common one is to enable the group to identify which of the answers are essentially the same albeit expressed differently, and which are completely different ideas. If necessary, a voting process can then be used to determine which direction to take next.

Converge

What voting can do is to demonstrate whether or not more dialogue is needed; whether a new solution to a problem has to be sought.

Within the world of facilitation, I have heard two definitions of consensus that I have found useful. The first is that consensus is taken to be when 80 per cent support a decision; considerably more than 50.05 per cent. The second, less easily measured, is when nobody leaves the room with the intention to undermine the decision. They might not be entirely happy, but are willing to accept that their view is not the

dominant view. From my experience this second circumstance occurs when two conditions are met. The first is when all feel that they have had the same opportunities to express their view as others, and the second is when all feel that they have been equally heard.

Currently, there are three techniques that I have found useful to help a group move through the dialogue process to an agreement. These are:

1. Multi-voting
2. Weighted voting
3. Graded agreement

The value of voting towards the end of a dialogue process is for all to see whether more talking is required. I have sometimes felt that people were still making a point whilst the need had passed. Using one of the techniques helps clarify the situation. What voting can do is to demonstrate whether or not more dialogue is needed.

Multi-voting

This works best where there is a long list of options. Initially everyone has a first cut at voting for, or ranking, all the options. The options that scored in the top 20 per cent are taken as confirmed. Those that scored in the bottom 50 per cent are taken out. The group votes again on the remainder in the middle.

Weighted voting

This helps spread results. Sticker dots are very good for this. Participants can place up to 1, 2 or 3 sticker dots on any one option. A variation involving holding hands up is where participants can hold 0, 1 or 2 hands up.

Graded agreement

Create four or five statements relevant to the particular situation. An example is:

1. I am fully supportive of this decision

2. I have a few minor concerns, but generally support this decision

3. I would support this decision with a few amendments

4. I cannot support this decision, and think we have to start again.

These can be stuck to the wall some metres apart from each other, and participants invited to stand under the statement closest to their views. Invite them to discuss what would have to change to move one step to acceptance. I have heard a variation of this process sometimes called Love it or Leave it.

The following are some examples of workshop designs based on these ideas and principles.

Strategic plan

I often use this running sheet, albeit usually with some small variation. In this instance the management committee of a recently refurbished village hall wanted to create a strategic plan. There were only four people in the workshop, which made the conversation processes easy but still required a logical structure. The approach was to help them clarify their common vision, and then develop strategies to achieve the vision through asking what the blockages might be. At this point I asked the group to identify the biggest challenge, or blockage (Figure 5.5). After a short discussion about the difference between an outcome and output, the participants worked in pairs to develop ways in which they might overcome the major issue. It was from here that the group decided to invite other groups in the town to use the hall (free of charge) to hold their regular meetings. My understanding is that this has evolved into the amalgamation of a number of the community groups.

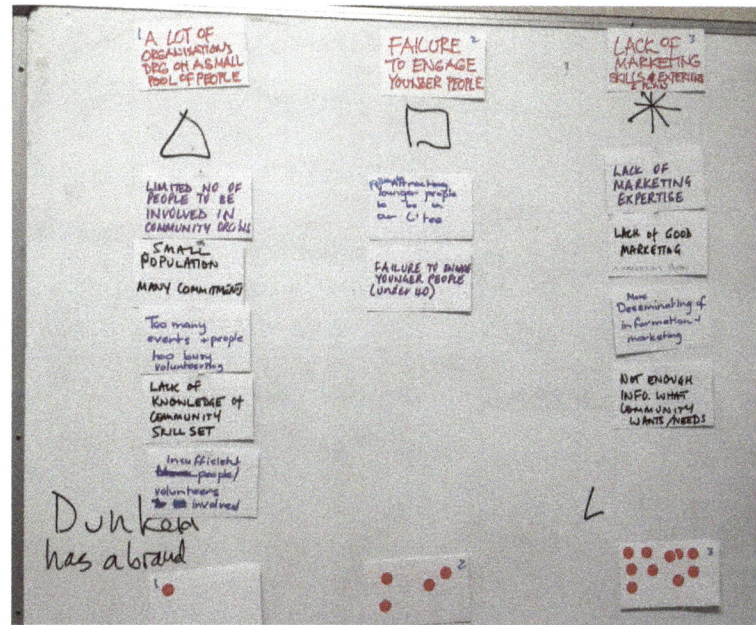

Figure 5.5 Named similar concepts relating to the underlying blockages confronting the centre.

Time	Mins	Outcome	Action	Design concept
1:00	5	Welcome	Introductions by all	
1:05	10	All comfortable	MB outline	
1:15	30	Common understanding of past	Journey Wall. With focus on what have been some of the things that have really worked well? Strategic plan.	Scope
1:45	20	Common Vision	Photo language: What would success look like?	Vision
2:05	20	Strategies	Card storm: What are the underlying blockages to acheiving the vision? Rank the top 4.	Strategy
2:25	20	Outputs developed	Outputs and outcomes quiz. Do easy-hard/effective-less effective analysis. Choose the outputs to progress.	Output
2:45	15	Evaluation and close	Focused conversation and evaluation sheets	

Team charter

Teams and groups of people sometimes have to express, discuss and agree on their own norms and behaviours. The real value of creating a team charter is in the discussions that the team have in building their own charter. This three-hour process provides a structured opportunity for participants to explore the breadth of what is a 'team charter'; discuss what is important to them; and, in an iterative manner, develop their own.

The conceptual framework is the Action Learning cycle, starting with scope and vision, followed with an iterative creative process. In this instance there was no requirement to create an action plan, though any document produced is always useful for the team to refer to at a later date as a mechanism for reflection and self-evaluation (Figure 5.6).

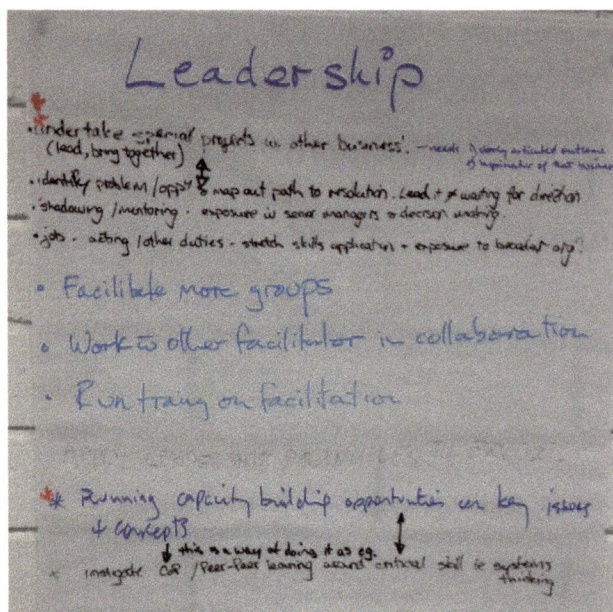

Figure 5.6 Words and phrases under the heading of 'Leadership'.

Time	Mins	Outcome	Action	Design concept
10:00	20	All comfortable	Welcome, introductions, outline.	
10:20	35	Participants get to see/ understand the breadth of a team charter.	Poster process. Examples of team charters.	Scope
10:55	15	Participants consolidate their learnings about team charter.	Triads. 2 x 5 minute groups of three. Discuss: What would be the key benefit of a team charter for this team?	Vision
11:10	40	Team Charter headings identified	Card Storm: What are the important things that should go into our team charter?	Diverge
11:50	20	Deconstruction: First part of iterative process.	Gallery process: What words and phrases need to go under this heading?	Groan zone
12:10	20	Notes re-formed into statements	Pairs/Triads: 1 x small group for each heading. Rewrite and smooth up the key words and sentences under each heading.	Converge
12:30	15	Evaluation and close	Focused conversation and evaluation sheets.	

Annual catch-up

This workshop was designed to be an annual catch-up of different teams undertaking essentially the same work across the state (Figure 5.7). It was the first day of a two-day event. Day 2 was a series of local field trips. The format was developed with the host team leader who wanted the event to be primarily a learning experience for all participants. To avoid a lot of slideshow presentations, we varied the processes to ensure as much interaction as possible. A particular challenge was encouraging individual participants to come to the workshop with Wicked problems rather than case studies. This required quite a lot of preparatory work with individuals.

The planning concept was a series of Diverge/ Converge pieces, with different techniques used to keep interest and variety.

Figure 5.7 The teams were all working on similar problems. This was an opportunity to come together and share experiences.

Time	Mins	Outcome	Action	Design concept
12:00		Lunch on arrival		
12:30	30	Welcome, outline, meet & greet		
1:00	10	All hear what policy group are doing	Specialist info 1: short talk by policy specialist	Scope
1:10	30	Relevant questions developed and answered	Specialist info 2: Q&A by table group	
1:40	30	All hear of eight specific topics relevant to their work	8 x 3 minute talks on relevant areas for the whole team (obtained earlier as being of most interest through survey monkey)	Scope
2:10	60	Participants explore further the five topics of most interest (e.g., relevance to their region etc.)	World Cafe (3 rounds 20 minutes)	Diverge/ Converge
3:10	90	Wicked problems from each region: six Wicked problems	Process dependent on variety of topics	Diverge/ Converge
4:40		End of day		

Small team planning session

This small team had to determine what they could realistically achieve for their annual program, given there was some 'have to do's', and reduced funding and personnel resources. The team members worked in different parts of the State, but knew each other through previous meetings and phone contact.

The concept was the LogFrame model, with the 'vision' already provided.

Time	Mins	Outcome	Action	Design concept
10:45	15	All comfortable	Welcome, introductions, outline 'reflectorium'. How are you doing? Anything that might be distracting you from the session that you'd like to tell us?	
11:00	20	All on same page with current situation	History Wall card storm. What have we done over the last 12 months?	Objective
11:20	20	Common appreciation of the past year's work	Focused convo. Write up on BP. What do you see? What are our strengths? What's generally working well?	Reflective
11:40	15	All understand where we're going	These are the desired outcomes. Evelyn sets out the context.	Vision
11:55	20	(not including time/money/resources) within the givens	Card storm in pairs. For each of the desired outcomes, what are the blockages?	Strategies
12:15	5	Outcomes and outputs discussion	Martin quiz	
	30		List of things we could do to achieve the outcomes. What concrete, achievable things can we do that build on our strengths and are working well to overcome the blockages to the desired outcomes?	Outputs
12:30	20		Lunch	
	20	Better understanding of the world	Easy/hard to acheve and less/more effective Binary analysis	Action Planning
	20	Being realistic...	What can we say that we can do? TPS	
	60		Action Planning: Milestones, who/what/when cards.	

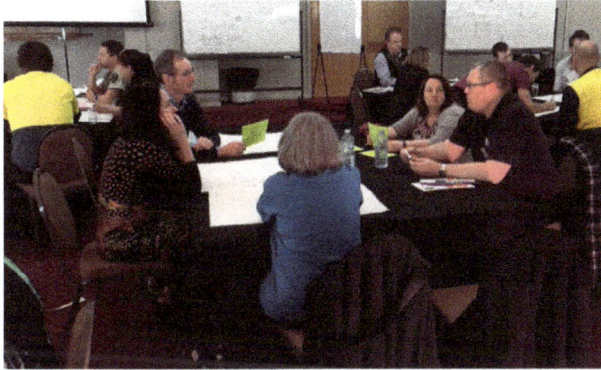

Fire recovery program reflection

This was an evaluation and reflection workshop for about 50 people (Figure 5.9). The workshop was to evaluate a difficult recovery program after the accidental escape of a planned burn.

Figure 5.9 In this instance an idea tested out was to ask participants separate out 'things that worked' and 'things that didn't work so well'.

Time	Mins	Outcome	Action	Design concept
9:30			Morning tea	
10:00	15	Welcome, introductions, outline	Welcome from senior public servant.	
10:15	15	Introductions, icebreakers	Pairs: 3 rounds. 1: What were you thinking on the way here? 2: I've been interested in emergency recovery since... 3: My hopes for today's workshop are...	
10:30	30	Understanding of activities in the critical period	History wall: What were the big events, the catalytic actions, the achievements, the pivotal points between these dates, e.g. meetings, announcements, reports?	Scope/ Objective
11:00	7	Reflection	Trios: Where were you most frustrated?	Reflection
	7		Trios: What were the big surprises?	
	7		Trios: A high point was....	
	7	Write up	Individually write up on supplied template: Template 1. Cut into three sections. Pin up.	
11:30	45	Interpretation: Key underlying items identified	Card storm with two colour cards: Green – what was underlying the events that worked well; Red – an event, thing, component, process, that caused problems, was not good. Then Templates 2 & 3: What lay behind the things that didn't work well, caused frustrations, created challenges?	Interpretive
12:15	30	Lunch		
12:45	15	After-lunch rejuvenation	Sociometric: 1) How long with the Department? 2) What has been the highlight?	
1:00	90	Recommendations.	World Café: Each of the key underlying themes (+ve & -ve) placed on a table. Probably about 8 –12. From this learning, what is your recommendation for future recovery efforts? 4 rounds of 20 minutes. Final tightening-up round.	Decisional
2:30		Space/ Evalaution	Individually: Complete evaluation forms	
3:00		End		

Transfer of surplus property

This was the third of three events to help the members of a small community decide if and how they might take on a lease of a government depot surplus to requirements.

The significant concept at play in this large-scale asynchronous process was Diverge/Converge. The first event was an Open House encouraging all to drop in and give their views about what the property could be used for. The second (Figure 5.10) was a World Cafe where they explored the various ideas identified in the first event. The third and final was a hybrid: recapping previous conversations, answering questions that had emerged, helping the various emerging groups listen to each other. Of particular note was how the Diverge/Converge process really did result in a transcendental solution: that is, a solution that nobody saw at the beginning of the process, but to which all stakeholders agreed at the end.

Being an asynchronous process, success was dependent on three key roles held by different people. Dave, the project owner, held the space

Figure 5.10 Table facilitators (or Cafe hosts) wore hazard caps, but everyone had power of the pen.

by not entering into the decision-making process, but ensuring that all understood that the community would decide. George was the in-place engagement person. He built relationships and encouraged all to attend the process events. I worked with George and Dave to design the process. In practice, this running sheet did not finish as planned, for rather than ranking the various contenders they decided to work together and develop an alternative model. We offered facilitation services, but these were not required.

Time	Mins	Outcome	Action	Design concept
1:00	15	All participants happy to start	Welcome, introductions, outline: Project owner	
1:15	40	All the difficult questions answered	Poster process: Answers provided to all the questions raised over the previous two workshops	Scope
2:05	10	What we're hearing is emerging	Specialist: Dave	
2:15	15	What we need to keep talking about – participatory analysis.	Sociometric. The two extremes are: the property must generate income; the property must be for community use. Where on the line do you stand? Listen to each other over the coming discussions.	Reflective
2:30	30	Greater understanding of the various proposals	Market place: Pecha Kucha for each group looking to take on the lease.	Interpretive
3:00	20	Tea		
3:20	15	Ranking	MB	Decisional
3:35	30	Summation: next steps	MB	
4:00		End		

LDSP learning review

In this quarterly reflection of a large donor aid project in Malawi, the conceptual framework was broadly the Action Learning cycle, incorporating ORID and LogFrame components to create the whole. The workshop commenced with looking at what had happened and reflection on this (the O&R of ORID). This was then extended using the LogFrame approach to create ideas that built on what went well.

Time	Mins	Outcome	Action	Design concept
9:00	30	All participants happy to start	Late start, welcome and introductions	
9:30	45	Common understanding of activities	History wall	Objective
10:15	15	Tea	LDSP learning review	
10:30	15	Hear each other	Over the last year, what went well? Table groups by key result area	Reflective
	15	Hear each other	Over the last year, what did not go well? Table groups by key result area (KRA).	
	15	Hear each other	Think Pair Share: Over the last year, what actions or activities would you do differently? Table groups by KRA. Top two actions on A4 sheets	Interpretive
11:15	30	A common vision for the next year	Human statues	Vision
11:45	45	Agreement on the underlying blockages to the vision	Card storm	Strategies
12:30	60	Lunch		
1:30	15	All ready to start again	Introduction bingo	
1:45	45	Activities to overcome the blockages	Gallery	Outputs
2:30	20	Cross-fertilisation of ideas	In mixed table groups. KRA leader to set out the context and get input from others on how to build on 'what went well'. Develop two ideas that build on what went well	Actions
2:50		End		

Assessment criteria for a trial project

Landholders are given permits to cull kangaroos on their property. An extension to a trial project to minimise the waste from this policy had been granted. However some key problems had been found, mostly around how to monitor and evaluate (M&E) the project. This workshop was for the extended team to develop M&E tools for the project. The vision (sufficient data is collected to inform evidence-based decision making on the commercial utilisation of kangaroo carcasses taken under the legislation) was a given, likewise the underlying blockages. Thus the concept was the LogFrame, but with the vision and blockages given. An additional one specific to this workshop was that the project manager would be

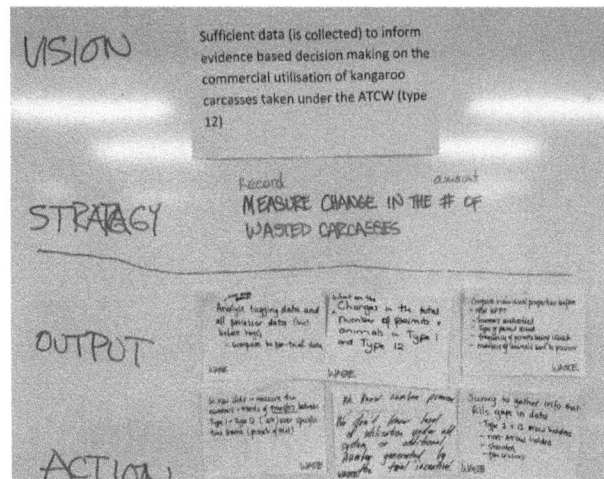

Figure 5.8 The vision and strategy were givens (with a slight tweak). The participants had to work out the concrete things they could do.

responsible to drive the actions identified by the extended team.

Time	Mins	Outcome	Action	Design concept
9:30	20	Welcome/introductions/late start		
9:50	45	Reflection: what's happened	Journey wall: What has happened, important, catalytic, etc.	Scope
10:35	10	Vision: confirm vision	Printed out. Questions for clarity.	
10:45	20	Ideas generated on how to overcome blockage 1	Noisy Round Robin: We don't know how to identify whether there has been a reduction in waste of carcasses.	Diverge/ Converge
11:05	15	Break		
11:20	10	Quiz: outcomes and outputs		
11:30	10	Check and rewrite		
11:40	30	Ideas generated to overcome blockage 2 (including check and rewrite)	Think Pair Share: We don't know how to assess the commercial viability of using kangaroo carcasses controlled through this program.	Diverge/ Converge
12:00	30	Ideas to overcome blockage 3 surfaced (including check and rewrite).	NRR: We don't know how to collect information to illustrate/inform whether compliance (with the relevant acts) is being achieved.	Diverge/ Converge
12:30	30	Lunch		
1:00	10	How long with organisation	Sociometrics: Relationship building	
1:10	20	Checking for outputs, i.e. concrete	One from each table	
1:30	15	Analysis of ideas/value to effort	How effective? How easy to implement?	Planning
1:45	5	Drivers: who and who on team		
1:50	20	Milestones	On Gantt chart	
2:10	60	Action	Who/what/when cards	
3:10	20	Evaluation	Reflection: what worked, what didn't	
3:30		End		

Line managers' meeting

This meeting of line managers from a sector of a large organisation was for them to unpack the results of an in-depth study into culture and behaviour within their sector.

Time	Mins	Outcome	Action	Design concept
10:30	10		Welcome, late start	
10:40	10	Participants welcomed & context	Bob	Scope
10:50	10	Participants welcomed & context	Jane	
11:00	10	Participants hear a personal testimony/ witness	Garry	
11:10	40	Individual learning	Poster process: Working collaboratively	
11:50	10	Culture: Participants articulate their own learning and understanding	Part 1) In table groups of about 6, individually and silently read at least 5 of the stories written by staff as part of the study.	Diverge/ Converge
12:00	20	Sharing experience	Part 2) In triads, participants share answers to questions: Thinking about your style in recognising and responding to these concerns, a) what could be your blind spots? And b) how could you resolve them?	
12:25	5	Commitment to change	Part 3) Individually make personal notes of: what to look for; how to respond differently.	Action planning
12:30	30	Refreshed participants	Lunch	
1:00	20	Energised participants	After-lunch engagement activity Speed dating. Upper case against the wall, lower case to match the letter. Three rounds of 5 minutes.	
1:20	15	Workforce: Participants explore the strategy and action plan 7 key elements	Gallery process. Two sets of 7 questions, each requesting ideas for implementation. Swap sides. View and rank.	Diverge/ Converge
1:35	10	ID top two actions to meet each target	Swap and look at other side. Each pair to rank top 2 ideas	Action planning
1:45	60	Wellbeing: key steps identified	To improve the health and wellbeing of our staff within the region. For each of the four key themes identified within by various surveys etc. Work – life balance Flexibility Succession planning Balancing emergency and regular work What clear actions could individual managers do to address each of these issues.	Diverge/ Converge
2:45	10	Wrap up	Focused discussion and end	

VCCCI

The Virtual Centre for Climate Change Innovation grants program was open for groups/ partnerships to apply for funding of innovative projects to tackle climate change. The concept was Action Research with the vision a given (successful grants will be innovative and collaborative). This was followed by an iterative process to help participants make connections with people they might find useful to work with.

Time	Mins	Outcome	Activity	Design concept
10.00	10	All feeling a bit more comfortable	Pairs: 2 rounds of participatory icebreakers: 'On the way here I was thinking…'; 'I've been interested in climate change since…'.	
10.10	10	Official start	Project welcome and outline of day	
10:20	10	Basic understanding	Specialist presentation: Outline of grant program (7 minutes)	Scope
10:30	30	All on same page.	By table group: develop questions (10 minutes), answers (20 minutes)	
11:00	20	Building relationships	By table group: What does innovation mean to you? What does a good collaborator look like? Call out key words and phrases. Two scribes to write up.	Scope
11:20	60	Ideas developed, relationships built further	Individually: Write up on cards your key areas of concern, or your adaptation or mitigation ideas.	Diverge/ Converge
			TPS (varient) (swap tables if necessary to find partner). Help each other clarify what he or she is saying.	Diverge/ Converge
			By table group. Help each other. Each person on the table is to choose a climate change problem/adaptation/ solution idea that interests them for now. ONE PER PERSON. Look for where the passion is!!	Diverge/ Converge
			Pairs: stand up and take your card to someone you have not yet shared your idea with – describe your issue/ project. Give it a name.	Diverge/ Converge
			Pairs: Swap, find someone else to describe your idea to – refining as you explain it again, flesh it out more, pitch it better. In what way is it innovative?	Diverge/ Converge
			Individually: Walk around the room holding your project card – look for others with a similar theme. Cluster together – name your common theme.	Diverge/ Converge
12:20	45	Happy participants	Lunch	
13:15	10	All brought back and ready for PM activities	Sociometric/lineup.	
13:25	40	Good quality start on projects	Groups of 3 (2 minutes/4 maximum)	
14:05	15		Helpers stay with project, Project owners move to look at another project	
14:20	10		Return to own project. Make changes	Decision
14:30	15		Any questions?	
		Thanks and Next steps	You will be invited to a second session	

Unsuccessful project evaluation

This was a relatively large, innovative project involving multiple partners. Unfortunately the project was not as successful as planned. The purpose of this workshop was to develop a coherent story that could be used as a 'lessons learned' document. The underlying workshop concept was the ORID framework.

Time	Mins	Outcome	Action	Design concept
10:00	20	All comfortable	Welcome and introductions. Round robin intro. Where have you come from today? How much knowledge do you have about this project?	
10:20	30	All remember what happened	In pairs: history wall (inc. video of plant; excitement in 2015).	Objective
10:50	10	Individual expressions	Triads: 'What really strikes me about this is...', one round and write up.	Reflection
11:00	30	Challenges identified	Gallery: contract management challenges? technical challenges? financial challenges? project management challenges? community engagement? surprises from left field? Top two identified.	Interpretation
11:30	20	Relationships identified	Rank challenges: big, not so big, etc. Venn diagram process; identify relationships.	Diverge/ Converge
11:50	30	Digging deeper. Particular incidents identified	Gallery process: for each subheading. What was the underlying story? In what ways did this impact the project, that is, contribute to our current situation? What do you really notice? What was the significance of the event? 2 x 3 triads, with individual write up	Diverge/ Converge
12:20	30	Lunch		
12:50	30	Learnings and recommendations drawn out	Learnings and recommendations for future projects. NRR	Decisional
13:00	20	Next steps	Next steps: What do we do with this information and learnings? Think Pair Share	Action Planning
13:20	10	Wrap up and evaluation	Evaluation forms	
13:30		End		

Online forums and workshops

As I was completing this book, the Coronavirus pandemic was just beginning. The small amount of experience I have had in participating or working with groups online suggests that the theory about how people collaborate on shared problems remains the same. The challenge is to

Time	Mins	Outcome	Action	Concept
10.00	15	All comfortable	Whole group. Who's in the room? Zoom housekeeping	
10:15	5	Welcome	Steve	
10;20	10	Traditional Owner (TO) presentation. Welcome to country and importance of the project to the TO's	T.O: Whole group	
10:30	5	All understand project background and parameters	Steve: Prepared ppt. on screen share	
10:35	10	This is Nature Kit: the background maps etc.	Rene: Screen share	info/ Objective
10:45	5	Nature Kit: mapping bio-diversity values	Rene: Screen share	info/ Objective
10:50	10	Participants discuss the information presented, and prepare questions of clarity to ask the team	Break out groups. Questions developed for clarity. Do you need more information? What is unclear about what we're asking of you?	Reflective
11:00	15	Answers are provided	Whole group. Screen share with Word Doc. as white board recording Q&A's. Zoom meetings, online forums and workshops.	Interpretive
11:05	5	Participants refreshed	Break	
11:10	7	Participants understand the request of them	Helen: Screen share presentation. How Nature Kit maps threats. Request for participants to start thinking about the threats that aren't already mapped	Into/ Objective
11:15	3	Participants understand the request of them	Steve: Screen share presention: How Nature Kit maps activities. Request for participants to start thinking about on-ground activities that aren't already mapped	Into/ Objective
11:20	10	Participants discuss the information presented, and prepare questions of clarity from the team	Break out groups: Do you need more information? What is unclear about what we're asking of you?	Reflective
11:30	15	Answers	Whole group. Screen share with Word Doc. used as a white board recording Q&A's	Interpretive
11:45	7	Description of way forward	Rene. Screen share: You can contribute by coming to another zoom meeting on how to draw a polygon, or you can send in the information for Dpt. to map. Phone us if you wish.	
11:50		Bring to a close	Steve: Whole group	
12:00		End		

find appropriate online technologies that can emulate the wonders of table groups, sticker dots and index cards. Over the years I have noticed many different platforms and apps that promise easy online collaboration. Whilst not in a position to make a critical analysis of them all, I have always been excited by the potential of the Zoom Screen Share and Breakout Room capabilities. A critical learning is that the length of time participants can spend in front of a screen is considerably less than when working with people in face-to-face workshops.

In my first workshop design in the new reality, the project team had already designed for themselves a full-day workshop to introduce a digital mapping tool to 30 participants. The focus was information delivery. They were looking for an online method to deliver the workshop. The challenge was to keep participants engaged online over a shorter period of time. The final running sheet prepared was based on the specialist information technique (see Ch. 4), in which the presenters kept their information succinct, clearly structured and within a maximum of 5 minutes. The presentations were then followed by small groups discussing the content. We also held a dress rehearsal, which contributed to success.

Summary

Creating safe spaces for individuals to express their own views, listen to others and subsequently create useful, sustainable decisions that they are willing to support is a really useful building block for strengthening complex social systems. Such safe spaces are generally workshops of between a few hours to a few days. How such workshops might interlink and build on each other is necessarily and by definition emergent.

How to scale up such concepts and processes is probably the big challenge. On the one hand I am conditioned by the realities of complexity, and how by definition it is not possible to design large-scale city-wide approaches or interventions. On the other, I find the interplay of the Action Research and the Diverge/Converge concepts so flexible, so robust, so adaptable, that I can see no reason why large-scale interventions should not be possible. The difference is between the traditional, or more institutional idea of scaling up, and what might be a response based on an understanding of complexity. In other words, it is not about conducting a pilot program, and then replicating the program at other situations, or at a larger scale. It is about approaching situations with a vocabulary of tools and techniques, and using them in a variety of contexts. We just have to do more of it.

CHAPTER 6

Theory in use: Reflections and learning

A critical part of understanding complex systems is to understand that it is not possible to understand them. This might sound illogical and even contentious, but it was one of the most useful realisations I have had.

Complexity is different to linear, complicated systems and problems because complex systems and associated problems don't obey the same rules. The temptation is to try to reduce the complexity into something tangible and solvable; Either that, or keep everything philosophically abstract, which has its own joys and limitations.

Learning challenges

My challenge is how to describe my reflections and learnings about working within complexity in a sensible, logical and coherent way when the experience has been anything but logical and coherent.

Another challenge is how to measure something that culturally and perhaps intrinsically we don't normally measure. Tame problems in complicated systems can be measured through counting the number of times something happens (like rejects in the manufacturing system, sales and sick leave rates). These are useful for measuring performance within a technical frame. Unfortunately we then use those figures to extrapolate what it means as an effect on the complex system. And the

connection is not linear. For example, the Ford Edsel bombed, the Ford Mustang was a sales success. But both are just cars, and maybe the impact in regards to making people happy had nothing much to do with the car as a product, but the time launched, the sales campaign, the mood of Americans at the time etc.

In Malawi I was astounded at the complicated computations developed by the international aid industry to determine the impact of development projects, but in the end they were still the equivalent of how other ages measured success: height of churches, size of empire, volume and value of products made and sold and so on. The link between outcome and output is always rubbery at best.

A further difficulty in making connections is that the linkage between an output or activity and its impact in the broader system is not consistent. Thus buying a new car might have once had a huge effect in how a person felt about life, but now it's just another household chore to fit in to a busy schedule (things to do: collect new car).

Additionally, the use of proxies or indicators of success to measure improvement and change in the broader system often becomes the outputs themselves. For instance, it might be determined that people are happy when they can buy a new car. The logic then becomes: therefore we should make more and more affordable cars. Chasing indicators thus becomes the goal, irrespective of whether or not the action actually achieves a positive outcome in the broader system.

Finally, there is language and how the words used to describe one thing can morph into being used for something completely different. An education colleague recently told me (in a cynical moment) that Action Learning means get a job, and lifelong learning means hurry up and get a job. Similarly, I am seeing and hearing ever more references to community engagement that have nothing to do with people being engaged in the decisions that will affect them.

The word 'consult' is just one example. Within a community engagement frame, it means gaining information from interested parties to inform the creation of a product (document, plan etc.). However within the traditional parlance of project management it means completing a product (often labelled draft) for others to comment on – a subtle, but very real difference in practice. Asking project managers about their consultation process often results in confusion. In real terms, the latter use often becomes 'selling', for after all the professionals will have put together a proposal that in their terms makes sense. It is usually only if there is outrage at the proposal, or if a team member is feeling very brave and questions the leader, that it is an effective way to good engagement practice. Thus even though there are definitions of such terms, popular use often wins out.

Reflecting about the work over time, I could tell you about the number of training workshops I've delivered, or the number of decision-making workshops designed and run, but to assess the impact in the broader system is considerably harder. When creating a building, irrespective of the architecture, a fundamental element of the design is to keep the rain out. I'm not sure if anyone would be genuinely happy with a leaky building. When creating spaces for people to work productively together, a fundamental design element is to create an environment that people find both useful (in terms of what they are trying to achieve) and, ideally, enjoyable or

at least not fractious and unpleasant. For it is when participants build positive relationships with each other that the linkages between the nodes of the social system will strengthen. My current thought is that the only consistent method to measure achieving such outcomes is through stories. A way to gather stories is to provide formal feedback forms for participants to complete (Figure 6.1). I'm aware that they are sometimes dismissed as 'happy sheets', and I'm conscious that I have a pretty good idea as to how a workshop is going, but I continue to ask for the forms to be completed for three reasons. It is a process for the participants' own reflection; to answer the question they have to think about their experience. If someone really does have something to complain about, it is far easier for them to write it than tell me in person. And finally, I continue to gain little insights from participants' comments.

Figure 6.1 The evaluation sheet I use for most workshops. Designed to elicit stories where possible, and most importantly an opportunity for participants' own reflection.

The four criteria I ask for a score and a comment on are:

1. How useful?
2. How enjoyable?
3. How well heard were you?
4. Did it help develop relationships?

Through these evaluation sheets, I generally get scores that average a little over 4/5 for most criteria in most workshops. However evaluation sheets are not the only source of insight, for stories are gathered in all kinds of ways. So what follows is a series of stories, stories about the things that seem to have worked and not worked for me when designing, implementing or just being part of participatory development processes. There are some instances when specific things did not work, but mostly it is always by degrees. In other words, degrees of success along a continuum.

A common starting point for any situation is the scoping phase of the AR/D process, this comprises both the analysis and visioning components. It seems as if it is not only rarely possible to get it right but according to Bob Dick, is a singular characteristic of the process. I have heard him say, 'Wherever you start will be wrong, so just start'.

Stories from the field

Story 1

Starting out as the neighbourhood improvement person on a public housing estate, I wanted to both engage with the community and discover what their big issues were. To begin, I asked a couple of friendly residents what they thought the big issues were on the estate. I arranged these onto a grid layout on a sheet of paper and for good measure put in boxes for 'other'. I clipped a strip of sticker dots to the sheet and put copies into the letterboxes of every house. I got a number returned, but it didn't really achieve what I was hoping for. Rather than

hearing all the voices, what I had done was to listen to a very small minority of people, just the two who had provided the initial issues. In addition, having boxes for 'other' on the voting sheet compromised the usefulness of the sheet as a vehicle to understand people's perceptions of the intensity of the problems.

What I had done was to mix up the brainstorming or 'hearing all the voices' part of the process with the dialogue part and even the deliberation part. Additionally, I had made the classic mistake of focusing on the deficiencies – the gap analysis – rather than trying to build on the very many strengths in the community.

Story 2

After learning from the pretty poor 'Vote for the Worst' survey, I ran a better process in a similar but different situation, working in outback Queensland. At the time my job description included the statement: 'Co-ordinate social, environmental and economic development using and demonstrating community planning processes and techniques'. There were a number of people in the community with ideas about how to develop the region, but this time I specifically wanted to find out everybody's ideas. The problem then was how to gather all those in a region covering 160,000 square kilometres with a population of just 30,000? My approach was the Quest for Regionally Significant Projects (QRSP).

Being a small community, I was able to access the local newspaper and radio station on a number of occasions and ask for all ideas, from anyone, in any form. This process worked well for a wide, geographically dispersed community, and was complemented by asking key people in the various clubs and societies (such as Rotary, Lions and ATSIC) to solicit ideas from their members. The question was clear, and didn't limit creativity by providing suggestions or examples. Ideas received ranged from build a kangaroo abattoir through to promote line dancing. I had set a target of getting 200 ideas, but after about three weeks and responses drying up at 65, I decided that was my new ambition. I am still a little disappointed that I only got 65 ideas from 30,000 people. I'm sure I could do better next time!

The Action Learning/Design process has two components in the initial scoping section: Analysis and Visioning. Helping a group set the vision is critical, yet also needs to be flexible.

Story 3

I was once asked to run a planning workshop for a particular team, and was told that there was a commonly accepted vision. This was provided but I had my doubts. At the appropriate place in the proceedings I asked the group to stand on a graded agreement line indicating their acceptance of the vision. It did not surprise me that the only one fully supporting the stated vision was the one who provided the brief.

I suggested that the group spend 10 minutes working in groups of three. Each trio was to create a human statue to illustrate success, and then play back their vision to the others. Every group produced a unique version of a very similar basic concept or vision. When I suggested that they write up their collective vision from the cards I had written from their descriptions, the answer was 'No need, we know it now'.

Story 4

At the other end of the spectrum concerning the amount of time allocated to visioning, combining a guided visualisation with a newsletter from the future is quite a lengthy activity, but can provide wonderful insights (Figure 6.2). It was from this vision that the group identified the need for the community-based organisation members to have literacy training. Fortunately, the project donors were sufficiently flexible to allow this variation. It was at this workshop that I got the feedback to the effect that 'Mr Butcher's games seemed childish, but were very useful'.

It may seem obvious, but in my experience the most significant failure at the scoping stage of a project, and a considerable impact on perceptions of process usefulness, comes when those with the power to implement a decision are not clear on the parameters of the discussion, that is, the negotiables and not negotiables on the topic. The project parameters as expressed by the negotiables and not negotiables might be developed and articulated by a project team, but subsequently they have to be agreed to by those with the power to sign off on any co-designed solutions. This is probably the most important part of any participatory project, as it sets up the frame in which others with less power can contribute. My observation is that failing to do this is the greatest source of contemporary participatory development failure. Asking or expecting people to develop solutions to a problem, and then having those solutions dismissed because they don't fit the frame of those with power, leads to cynicism, a breakdown in trust and further depletion in human capital and the strength of the human system as a whole.

Story 5

In a project concerning fishing[1] on a beach, one of the negotiables determined by the project team was 'the use of the beach'. This led to an expectation amongst sectors of the community that commercial fishing from the beach could be halted. Unfortunately the team was not aware that at a higher level an agreement had already been made with the fishing industry[1] that commercial fishing would remain. Without this information, the focus of the conversation was how this use could be either stopped or maintained. If known, the conversation could have been on when, where, under what conditions commercial fishing might be carried out. As it gradually emerged that commercial fishing would continue, there was considerable outrage about not being heard. If the engagement framework or project parameters are not clear and transparent, people feel that

---

1   The specific industry changed.

CU Kuphunzira

Volume 10 Issue 4 April 2020

Concern Universal Malawi Newsletter

After hearing about the UN award for being the most liveable area in Malawi, I visited Thyolo last week to see for myself what it was all about. Honestly, I was amazed at the transformation since I worked there.

I saw TA Mphuka transformed into a a well developed area. There is 100% water supply coverage and the economic wellbeing of the people. There was a good rural road network for easy travel.

I found:
• Good forest reserves all over the TA
• 100% food security and livestock sources
• Availability of secondary schools in the area

I heard stories about how there was high self dependency & goc partnerships happening in TA Mphuka
A CBO revolving fund assessed by the community
A livestock pass-on program working efficiently
Established advocacy and GBV committees.

I felt that Mphuka to be a model TA in Thyolo as well as a bre.. basket.

CU Kuphunzira

Volume 10 Issue 4 April 2020

Concern Universal Malawi Newsletter

After hearing about the UN award for being the most liveable area in Malawi, I visited Thyolo last week to see for myself what it was all about. Honestly, I was amazed at the transformation since I worked there.

I saw aged people and youngsters who were looking healthy and well nourished and their dressing sent a message about people who are now outside the poverty trap. New school buildings and other structures were seen from a distance appearing as a busy trading centre with electricity. As I was passing through the village I saw a lot of iron and thatched houses with satellite dishes here and there.

I heard stories about a lot of pupils going to school and that there is compulsory primary education as there are now by-laws put in place. I also heard stories that where I saw a trading centre was a place that used to be Mylenga CBO but it has developed to become a local NGO and other rooms built by them are used as shops and local salons. I heard that most families are living peacefully and gender based violence is a thing of the past.

I felt proud that what used to be a poor Mphuka area is now a developed area where people are food secure, practicing all year round agriculture due to irrigation.

CU Kuphunzira

Volume 10 Issue 4 April 2020

Concern Universal Malawi Newsletter

After hearing about the UN award for being the most liveable area in Malawi, I visited Thyolo last week to see for myself what it was all about. Honestly, I was amazed at the transformation since I worked there.

I saw a well dressed, well nourished elderly woman walking majestically long the better road. Not far behind her were her grand children coming from a well built secondary school and they were all walking towards their iron roofed house surrounded by a granary full of harvested maize, improved sanitary facilities, goat and pig kraals full of livestock and just 200m there was a borehole. All the hills of Mphuka were covered by trees and the ecology and been reverted to it's natural state with happy people benefiting from forest products e.g.: honey.

I heard stories about the CBO's having grown into local NGO's and the network coordinator is now a councillor, representing the people of his area and has recently been elected chairman of Thyolo council. I also heard of 30 families formerly involved in gender based violence had bought motorcycles and were working to help other families change. They are role models of T/A Mphuka. Almost 50% of the CBO's have qualified and have Diplomas in Accounting. Every household in T/A Mphuka is using energy efficient stoves and the neighbouring T/A's have emulated the good practice in T/A Mphuka.

I felt humbled to have contributed to this change in the area having worked under the Mphuka shared futures project. I was fired up, invigorated motivated, and encouraged to do more if given another chance in another community in another area.

I was still in the euphoria of the goodness I had seen, heard and felt when it was time to say my goodbyes to Mr Chidakwa Mbeue the elected chairman of District Council, formerly the CBO Network Coordinator of Mphuka.

Figure 6.2 Three newsletters from the future developed by the three table groups. This two-part process commenced with a guided visualisation process..

they have been coerced into a sham process. At some point they realise that what they have been saying, what they have been talking about, what is important to them, is not going to make a difference. From this builds increasing cynicism about process and further breakdown in the linking capital between the nodes of the system.

Story 6

A colleague and I were asked to develop a stakeholder management mechanism for a significant work group. The project owner gave authority for any of his busy staff who wished to be involved in a workshop process to do so. Unfortunately we failed to identify his negotiables and not negotiables concerning a solution at the start of the project. At the end, when presented with the group's approach to the problem, he went through with a red pen crossing out items he didn't like and inserting the activities that he thought were missing.

Story 7

A further example was an inter-agency approach to address domestic violence in an outback town. Whilst the group believed that they had the imprimatur to develop their own solutions, the project owner (who was based in another town 200 km away) had simply made her own decision as to how to spend the money. The outcome was a disappointed and deflated group of people.

Story 8

In another, larger project, 600 people (including myself) attended a two-day America Speaks workshop to determine how a segment of the local authority's social services budget should be allocated. A few days after the event, the mayor thanked the participants for their work, but advised how council would in fact allocate the budget.

In contrast to the failures I've witnessed with the project parameters not being clear, and on a positive note, where there is clarity there are success stories with great outcomes.

Story 9

A project team responsible for developing the management structure for ground water in the state were not sure whether their project had the capacity to change existing legislation. It took them some weeks to obtain an answer (No), but it was then possible to legitimately engage ground water users in discussions about future management processes with this limitation absolutely clear. In one of their workshops, a participant expressed his amazement and appreciation that the government public servants were asking his input into solving the problem, and not just presenting their solution. The team's iterative and inclusive process resulted in a solution that they acknowledged could only have come from the process used, but which also resulted in it being signed off in record time.

Story 10

A different kind of example of boundary clarity was the project owner who enabled a small rural community lease a government depot that had become surplus to requirements. The disparate groups that had their eyes on it were expecting him to make a decision on who would be granted the rights to use the facility. Whilst he later admitted that to refrain from giving any advice or suggestions was the hardest thing to do, he understood the importance of remaining neutral and advising that the community would make the decision. To enable this, he arranged for those within the organisation with the skills to design and implement a facilitated process that supported the community members to go through the Diverge/Converge decision making process. He was also responsible for ensuring that the complex leasing arrangements necessary for the final community-owned solution were achieved within the bureaucracy. The role of champion requires a very special skill set, but not necessarily that of designer. In current parlance, the role is closest to that of leader. Not a leader in the old sense of being able to rally the troops or have the numbers, but a person whose vision includes an awareness of complexity and the strategic desire to create the space for others to have control and choice in the process of growth and change. These people can be found at all levels of organisations, and in all kinds of roles across the community, but within a government structure would be referred to as the project owner. If they don't have this view of their role, then a participatory approach cannot work.

As well as finding processes with clearly defined parameters in which they can participate useful, people often find them enjoyable.

My observation is that, when provided with a structured process, people enjoy working together. It is when the structure breaks down or is inappropriate that participants become stressed and unhappy. When consideration is given to the working environment itself, the challenges of overcoming difference can be transformed from something antagonistic and fractious to being enjoyable and positive. I have observed both as a participant and as a practitioner that what helps the process is for the facilitator to provide the minimum amount of context for an activity, followed by instructions on what people are to talk about (best framed as a question), where to talk, and for how long.

These instructions might be framed in a variety of ways. For example, 'This is a three-part process. To start with I would like you to individually think about (question) for two minutes.' I have found consistently that the workshops getting the highest enjoyable scores are those where the participants have done as close to 100 per cent of the talking as possible.

Story 11

I once ran a small 90-minute workshop as part of a larger, more formally arranged two-day conference. The conference was generally well received, and the speakers considered worthwhile. I found it interesting that as well as getting good scores across the board on the feedback sheet, a number of the workshop participants explicitly stated it was the most enjoyable part of the conference. I had only told them what to talk about and for how long.

Story 12

Along with reflecting on how participants seemed to enjoy everyday structured workshops, I decided to test this observation in a different context. To do this, I developed a workshop process for participants to determine the environment for happy humans. After a few trial runs with friendly groups, I ran the process as a fringe arts festival event. The participants in this instance walked in off the street (so to speak), not even expecting to be involved in a participatory decision-making process. It didn't win any awards, but my primary evaluation question of the 10-12 unrelated people attending each session was 'To what extent did you enjoy the 75 minutes of session time'. In all cases, there was a high level of enjoyment expressed.

As described earlier, it is the interaction of the Action Learning and Diverge/Converge models that produces meaningful processes. A critical component of the Diverge/Converge model is the idea of transcendence.

Story 13

To achieve a transcendental solution, the nature of the problem has to be described in more than a yes/no format. I live in a city where a group of residents were taken through a three-day facilitated process to decide whether the mayor should be voted from within the council ranks (such as the Westminster system) or separately (as in the US presidential system). After three days of rumination the group was still split 50/50. Individuals had swapped sides, but the proportion remained effectively the same. The idea of dialogue in the Diverge/Converge model is a reflection of the ambiguity of complexity, and that there is no one right answer, only an answer that those affected are willing enough to support. In this instance, there was no room to develop a completely different solution to the either/or frame of the question. The act of dialogue is to generate a new solution beyond the simplistic ones initially proposed and lobbied for, a solution that reflects all the different values and idiosyncrasies of real people, creating and making a choice that transcends the banal. It resides in the understanding that today's world needs more than a debate.

Daniel Kahneman in his book *Thinking, Fast and Slow* explains how we tend to fall in love with our own ideas, even if they are wrong, and then feel compelled to justify them and, even better, get them accepted by others. This means that most of us will use whatever it takes to persuade others that our view is right. The world of intentional communities is littered with failed dreams built on decision making based solely on dialogue. The intention is to reach consensus, but that rarely genuinely occurs through dialogue alone. The reality becomes one of debate, point scoring and posturing, usually with all parties locked in the drama triangle. The alternative offered by the structured deliberative workshop environment is that those involved might come with their opinions, but by actively participating together in the problem solving process have the permission (or freedom) to shift and morph their thinking and collectively develop a transcendental solution to the problem.

Story 14

A striking example I recall of the idea of transcendence in practice was a group wanting to improve the sporting facilities of their small outback town. At the start of the workshop series at least one of the participants was convinced that the answer was to construct a large indoor sporting facility, suitable for seven-a-side soccer, netball etc. After participating in the analysis of all the sporting facilities in the town, ranking them according to quality of facilities (Figure 6.3), and numbers of people

Figure 6.3 Discussing the results after ranking the quality of facilities on a scale of 1-5.

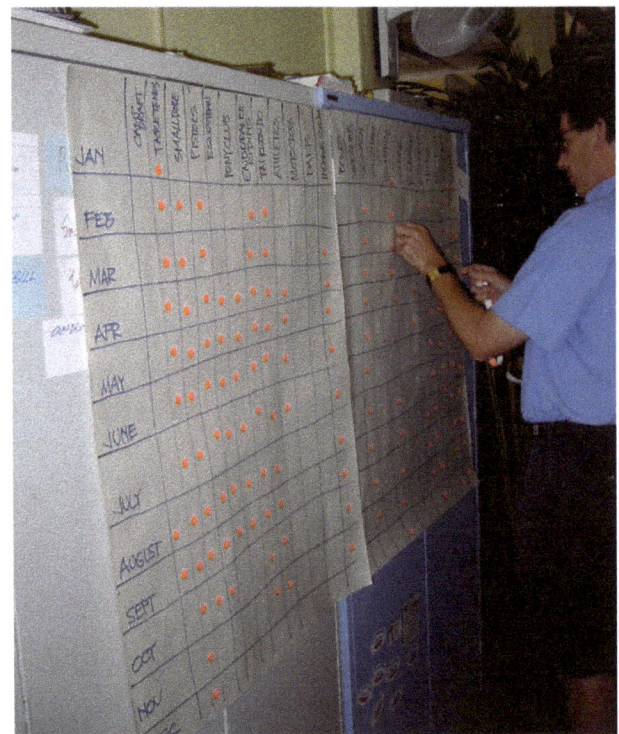

Figure 6.4 Mapping frequencies of use of sporting facilities in the town

using them (Figure 6.4) it started to emerge that what would make the most difference would be to top-dress the touch football ground and build a spectator mound along the edge. After they had decided this I almost asked the participant what had changed his mind. Fortunately I stopped myself, because it didn't matter. Of more importance was the observation by the Shire Economic Development Advisor that a consultant would have charged a lot of money for the research they had done collectively.

Story 15

Another small but successful example of the idea of transcendental solutions concerned the relationship between government staff responsible for meeting planned fuel reduction burning targets and the local tourist industry. In this instance there was a sufficiently high level of trust between the organisers and each of the two groups that they were willing to meet in a Bi-focal workshop process. We ran the process precisely according to the script. After each of the groups had listened to each other, it was identified that a significant issue that could be addressed was for the planned burn team to inform the local tourist information office when a burn was cancelled at the last moment. Apparently it was aggravating for the tourist officers to have told customers throughout the day that there would be smoke in the area and not to be alarmed, and to then hear back that there was none in the area because the burn had not gone ahead.

Story 16

I was recently involved in a dispute between two branches of a government department concerning responsibility for a particular segment of work. After using some participatory analysis techniques to explore the context of this work, a solution was developed. In reviewing the solution, all were satisfied with the majority of the plan. However there was one critical element that was causing contention. Neither wanted to take ownership of this element, and both thought it was the other branch's responsibility. It was at this point that I used a shortened version of the Bi-focal technique. In this process I set up chairs in two circles, but it was only necessary for each group to speak for 10 minutes each. Both sides were able to articulate their concerns on the matter and be heard by the other. I then reiterated that what was required was a transcendent solution, a solution that

would meet both their requirements. We broke for lunch, the participants stood around talking and eating sandwiches, and after 20 minutes a solution was provided by a participant. After a short period of further discussion and detailing, we were able to proceed to checking acceptability through a graded agreement process.

My learning is that clear project parameters and structured processes help considerably towards people feeling useful, valued and positive enjoyment. As well as clear project parameters leading to such outcomes, it is the micro details that assist in this. A structured process is more than just an application of participatory design concepts, it is also how it is constructed in real time. Two critical micro components are:

1. Building relationships
2. Being heard.

Relationships are a vital component of achieving good outcomes from Wicked problems. It is a critical element of any workshop or event. When people get to know a little more about each other, have shared a problem together or have worked together on developing a solution of some kind, they build a little linking social capital between them. I find it always a challenge to convince project managers of the need to have time simply for people to get to know each other better.

It takes time and gradual disclosure to build sufficient trust in another before being willing to open oneself to scrutiny. As well as using a variety of icebreaker-type processes to get people to talk to each other, it is also possible to design in processes that both actively help relationship building as well as form part of the workshop content.

To achieve this, I will often use variations of the ORID framework with sociometrics. I might start a workshop asking participants to stand in a line according to how far they have had to travel to get there. This is nice and objective, and not particularly confronting. Once in the line, I might ask them in turn to state their name, where they've come from, and something that they like about the their home town.

Whilst structures such as ORID are useful, the reality of complexity is that designing a meaningful process for a group to work together does not have to be linear. Thus I might start with a sociometric activity such as described, and then move to something like a History Wall exercise. A History Wall itself provides an opportunity to share individual understandings of what has occurred in the past. From there, it might be appropriate to move to a visioning exercise, again a collective activity. However, after a break or lunch, I might run an exercise such as introduction bingo, which is all about the group building a better understanding of itself. Such an exercise after a break is also useful to allow for the late returners. It doesn't matter too much if some miss the exercise, and at the same time it's important to honour those who return at the agreed time.

Story 17

Using the History Wall (Figure 6.5) technique is a great way for different people to express their understanding of a project or neighbourhood as well as build relationships. I have noticed this to be especially the case when working in geographic communities. When working on

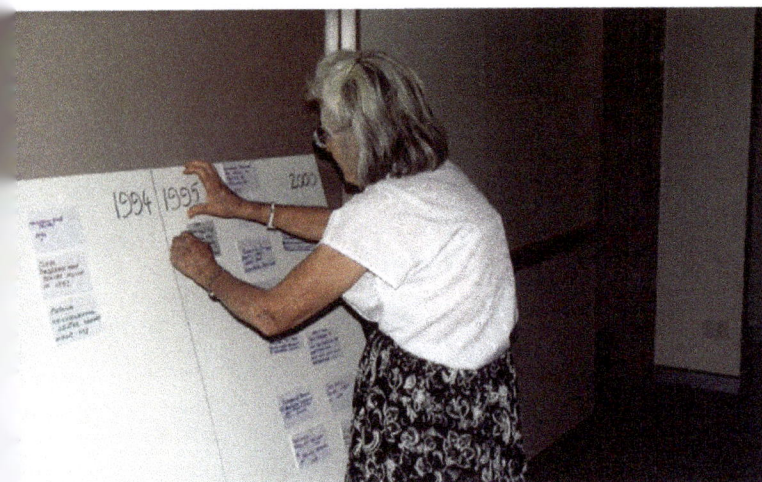

Figure 6.5 History walls offer an opportunity for participants to build relationships as well as sharing information.

public housing estates there was always a collective nod of understanding when a participant put up a card that related to the introduction of heroin onto the estate.

This relationship building aspect of the technique is also the case when there has been a number of staff working on different elements of a large project.

Story 18

In Malawi, it was common for projects to have a quarterly reporting workshop. Traditionally this was based around a series of individual Power-Point presentations. Changing to a History Wall format resulted in participants being engaged on the day (not busy preparing their own presenta-tion) and being able to see the linkages between the different components of the project. It was also a lot faster, and provided more time for gen-uine reflection and learning conversations be-fore planning the next quarter's activities.

Building relationships is part of successfully working within a complex system; being heard also has multi-dimensional characteristics.

Within a workshop process itself, people want to be listened to, but for different reasons. Bob Dick refers to the world comprising two types of people, introverts and extroverts. He defines introverts as those who think before they speak, extroverts as people who need to speak to think. Thus a key component of feeling engaged in a project or workshop is having the opportunity to express one's ideas, issues and concerns. From the scores and comments provided my observation is that the critical element is exactly that, and who is doing the listening not so important.

As a participant, I find it difficult to express my views in front of many more than four other people. Whilst most people are extroverts within Bob Dick's definition, some people are more self-confident and less shy than others. I'm not one of the self-confident ones. It is not my idea of fun when someone stands at the front of a room with a microphone and says, 'Let's have a conversation'. There might be one or two brave souls who proffer their observations on the topic, but most of the air time is taken by the person with a microphone.

Story 19

The whole-group discussion format only satisfies the confident and articulate. I recall an instance at a meeting of about 30 participants (agency staff and Indigenous people) where the inexperienced facilitator hired for the occasion started off by asking how people might want to discuss the topic, either in table groups or as a whole group. Almost immediately two confident males demanded a whole-group discussion, which resulted in the two dominating the rest of the time allocated.

It was not fun nor useful, nor did it help to build relationships between the participants. Regrettably I have experienced more than a few instances where those with institutional or community status have insisted on having a whole-group discussion. The result is always less than what might have been possible.

It is from these experiences that I consistently avoid theatre-style seating arrangements and the large circle of chairs. Both these layouts promoting the potential for a few to dominate the time. The latter is particularly gruesome – wondering what witty/insightful/original comment to make as your turn gets closer and closer and...the result is...stressful...and not listening to any of the other participants.

Cabaret (or Cafe) style layouts, and plenty of opportunities for participants to stand in pairs or trios, work well.

As mentioned, I find the most reliable and useful way for people to both express their ideas and feel heard is to have them written down. In large asynchronous processes, it is even more important that ideas, comments and concerns are written down. When briefing assistants attending Open House and Listening Post

events, I emphasise how they might have a great conversation with a member of the public, but unless what they've heard is written down (immediately, and confirmed with the individual) they have just wasted three people's precious time: the time of the person giving their views, their own time, and the time of the next person who has to hear them being repeated. But sometimes it does help to have a verbal reinforcement or interpretation of the written information.

A disadvantage of the World Cafe process is that it either takes a number of participants away from being able to participate in all the conversations, or requires a large number of resources (non-participant table facilitators) to be the cafe hosts and conveyors of meaning from one conversation to another. A disadvantage of the Noisy Round Robin process is that the words on the sheet of paper have to stand on their own. Those reading won't have the benefit of verbal explanation. I have on occasion overcome this dilemma with a modification to the World Cafe process (where the paper stays on the table and the people move) by having one person from the group hold back for two minutes to explain to the next group what they have written. After this two minutes, that person moves on and catches up with their group at the next table. At the next change, a different participant takes on the role. Just make sure to allow more time for each round.

I find 'report backs' from small group discussions are not useful. General report backs on a discussion are always taken over by the most powerful in the group, and become more a platform for their points of view rather than any kind of useful consensus.

This is different to when small groups have been instructed to conclude a topic of conversation. They are not reporting back on the discussion, but on their final decision. This might be a few words or a sentence.

Top-down and bottom-up frameworks

On reflecting on the two standard processes I use, that is the ToP/LogFrame process for where there is a bottom-up nature to finding an appropriate output that will lead to achieving a desired outcome, and the Stakeholder engagement planning process for where the output has already been determined, these have both been robust approaches.

When using the ToP/LogFrame sequence, I sometimes start with asking the group to develop a vision, but equally (if not more so) I find an outcome has already been set. The problem is that a project team is not quite sure where to go next.

Story 20

An interagency team was struggling to get collaboration (defined as where partners work together to develop solutions to complex problems) to actually occur in its project. It took some time to develop a workshop brief, which started with those attending identifying the top seven most important project outcomes from 20 earlier identified by a consultant. Using simple workshop processes the participants worked through the ToP process to identify useful outputs to achieve each of these, and within three hours produced two clear ways forward for the team.

When helping a team determine who they need to engage and in what manner, I consistently find the four-step process leading to a strategic engagement plan useful. A few stories follow.

Story 21

After a large fire with considerable property losses, a government team had to replace a water pump. The pump was not owned by the State, and its installation did not comply with regulations. However it had been used (and damaged) as part of the fire-fighting efforts and a ministerial commitment had been made to replace it. Initially the project team had to determine two critical non-negotiables. These were 1) that the state might fund the replacement pump, but was not interested in owning it, and 2) that the replacement had to comply with regulations. The stakeholder analysis process identified that there were only three people who really had any stake or interest in the project. A facilitated one-hour session with those three culminated in an agreed way to progress.

Story 22

When the stakeholders were analysed, it was realised that a good idea for a $60 million project would be almost impossible to implement. The funding was redirected.

Story 23

The project manager responsible for investigating the legal aspects of privatising a government service identified that the broader community would be a stakeholder. In developing the engagement plan the team realised that in fact it was only three lawyers and two academics that would actually be interested in their part of the project.

In a similar vein, a group looking into creating a trail along a river bank realised that they'd been trying to collaborate with the wrong stakeholder.

The big learning

From all of this work, one of the biggest learnings has been the relevance and importance of enabling people go through the Diverge/groan zone/Converge process at each step of the Action Learning/Design cycle. In practice it is rare for this to occur in a coherent, pre-planned manner.

Currently, my observation is that once moving beyond the idea of a single person making the decision, there are three common ways in which decisions are made that engage with others. The first is where that person (or agency)

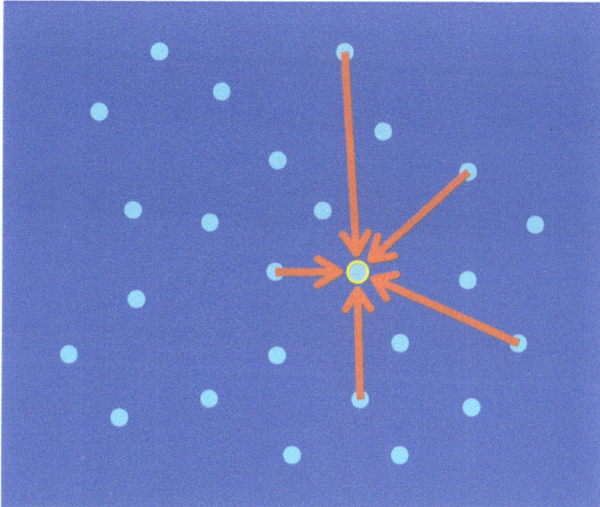

Figure 6.6 A common situation where the decision-making body consults with others prior to making the decision.

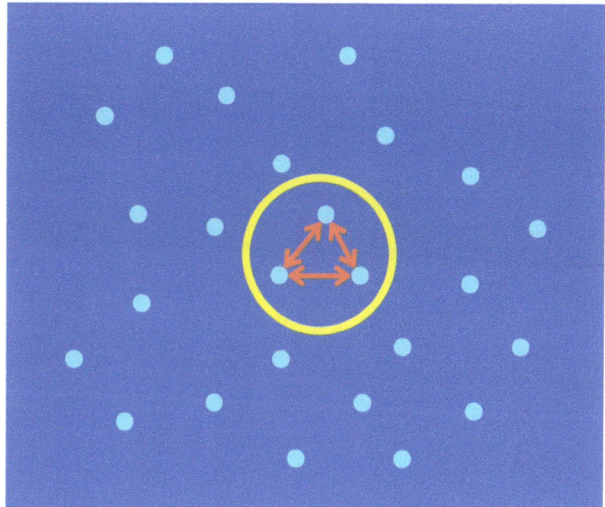

Figure 6.7 Another common situation where the decision-making body comprises a small group that make a collective decision on the part of others.

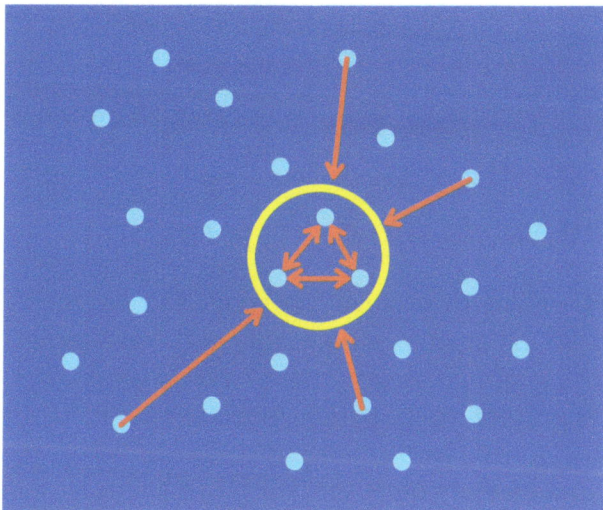

Figure 6.8 A less common situation where the small group of decision-makers (whether individuals or agencies) consult other stakeholders prior to making the decision.

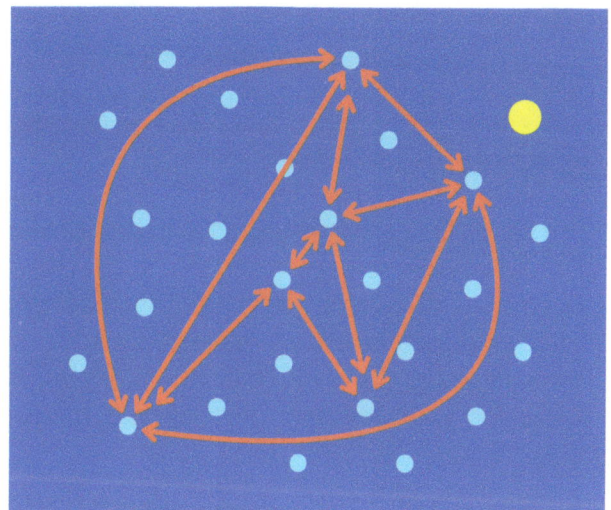

Figure 6.9 A different approach, where the powerful individual or agency facilitates a process in which those with a stake in the decision are taken through a process of transcendental problem solving.

consults others with a stake in the decision (Figure 6.6). The second is where a small number of people, sometimes in a workshop process, work collaboratively to make a decision. Sometimes this group is elected to do so; sometimes it is a work team, and in some instances they are even chosen at random (Figure 6.7). In either case, it is only a small group (or individual) that goes through the transcendental process. A modification to this situation is where that core group consults other interested parties prior to making a decision.

This is becoming a little more common, but still disenfranchises many others (Figure 6.8).

For me, the breakthrough concept underpinning the emergence of the social age is the shift in the idea of leadership. Good leadership is increasingly being defined as the capacity to describe the parameters and at the same time enable others to make decisions. Poor leadership is giving instructions and micro-managing (Figure 6.9).

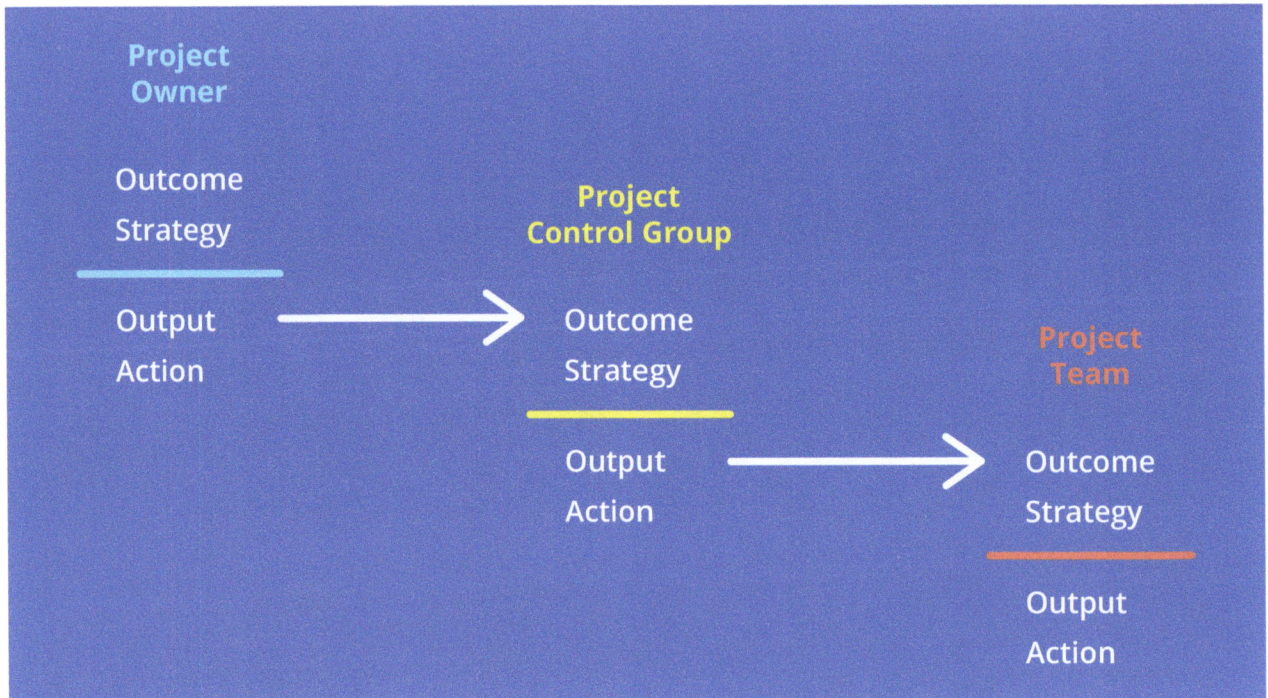

Figure 6.10 An Institutional structural model for both bottom up and top-down programs. This can be within the parameters of almost any broad-scale development objectives, such as climate change adaptation, education, social programs, land use/maintenance.

It is rare to find a formal organisation or group of people that is not organised in some form of hierarchical structure. However, increasingly projects and decisions are having to be made across structures, and with individuals or groups of people who are not part of any formal structure.

Our contemporary social construct is that a formal hierarchical structure is the norm for decision making and subsequent implementation. The top-down, bottom-up frameworks can help provide clarity to roles and responsibilities at different levels or organizational structure, in particular by applying the LogFrame logic model to the established project management layers (Figure 6.10).

What I see possibly emerging is a culturally accepted structural model where the powerful one (whether individual or agency) acts as facilitator to enable all those with a stake or interest in the outcome to be taken through the Diverge/Converge process.

Towards the next iteration

If we are to achieve the goal of more people learning from experiencing the Action Learning or Design paradigm, there have to be multiple opportunities for people to experience it. Whilst there are diverse methods to do this within the structure of contemporary government institutions, I can see two potential ways. Both depend on working with the willing, and building on existing strengths in any given situation.

What this means is a fundamental reconsideration of how power is expressed in society and is not something that will occur overnight. It will be a process of change and growth. The probability is that it will emerge through considerable chaos and discord. The art will be how to foster and enable a different reality to happen artfully and with consonance.

The reality of government institutions is that they are based on forms of hierarchy. One way in which this structure could be modified to work better is to more formally align the layers that currently exist within the institutions with the LogFrame concept. Each layer would have specific responsibilities that enable the subsequent layer to develop solutions within defined parameters. This structure could work for both top-down and bottom-up conceptual frameworks.

The first is through geographically based projects and programs where the approach is to enable local people to develop projects that respond to their local geographically relevant, visions, issues and concerns. The second is large-scale regional or national projects and programs where the output is usually a policy or legislation. In this instance it is about engaging communities of interest in the development of the desired output

In both cases, the established organisational structure can be adapted to accommodate a participatory approach in both top-down and bottom-up scenarios. The organisational structure might be the same for any other project: a senior bureaucrat as a project owner, a project control board and a project team. It is the skills deployed, the roles played and the relationships between the individuals within the structure that is different to current practice. These skills and roles can be found within the workshop environment, and then used as a development model for larger, wider, inclusive processes.

For instance, a workshop facilitator has four key roles.

1. Designing the process
2. Holding the space for the participants to do the talking
3. Encouraging participation through checking in on groups and keeping time
4. Writing up what is agreed.

In large-scale asynchronous processes, each of the roles could be carried out by different people, and would generally require more than one person. Thus a key component of a

successful large-scale participatory program would be to have the right skill sets and roles available, and at the right time.

Of critical importance will be the champion with strong enough credentials within the existing power structure or authority to hold the space. In the World Bank Participation source book, project managers were advised that if the minister of their particular development focus was not interested in a participatory approach, find another champion.

The project steering committee would ideally comprise those able to design a process suitable for the context. With this in mind, the key professional personnel would be participatory designers/facilitators, not engineers or health professionals or personnel from any other technical discipline. These key personnel will have the skills of facilitators, and able to translate the skills into asynchronous processes. The skill is the ability to both hold the space and provide the techniques for others to talk and listen to each other at each part of the participatory design process.

Because the role of these facilitators is to advocate that all voices be heard, facilitators should be recruited from a group that does not have a stake in the issues or geographic neighbourhood. This might well mean simply not being from the local area. It is too difficult (and unrealistic) to expect someone to be properly neutral when having a vested interest in the decision. I have tried literally to have two hats that I would swap depending on whether I was participant or facilitator. This is not only hard work but makes the role of being a neutral person in the eyes of all other participants difficult. How that person is paid and by whom, however, is not an issue. It is how they behave that is critical.

Finally, there is a need for people who can make connections and build relationships with others, people who can build the trust that getting involved in the development process will be useful, safe and potentially even enjoyable. All they can do is to be available and known within the community, encouraging participants with a stake in the issue to participate. It is a critical role, but it can only support a well-designed process, not rescue a poor one.

Technical experts might be needed at times within a project, but the role should be advisors, not project drivers. The role is best described in the 'planning for real' process. In this process a large model is built of the local neighbourhood, and community members modify it and change it. The technical specialists in the workshop wear large badges stating their professional expertise, for instance structural engineer, landscape designer. During the workshop they are only allowed to speak when asked a direct question.

Funding and resources

The scale and topics of projects and programs that people are likely to be interested in will be diverse. Often they will be very small. I worked with a small group on a public housing estate over a period of six months. Their vision was people on the estate getting on well together. The project they came up with was to invite the leaders of each of the identified cultural subgroups to cook a meal for each other. Total project cost: $300.

There are many examples of small-scale collaborative development projects undertaken with almost no money. However if there is a desire to actively promote a participatory inclusive approach to development, whether within a top-down or bottom-up frame, having resources available to implement projects makes a difference. There are always stories of those that achieve tangible results despite all odds, but more commonly good enough development goals (either personally or with others) are achieved when there is access to discretionary funds. The poor cannot afford to take risks. Only when backs are against the wall does this occur, and that situation is not one that allows for failure.

Figure 6.11 An example of a very useful development HQ. The building had a large space for workshops, together with smaller spaces (originally offices) that could be used as breakout rooms. Also kitchen and toilets.

Thus I would suggest that such an emergent process and approach will be found in situations when the following preconditions are met.

1. There is effective political support for a participatory process. No hidden agendas, and clearly defined project and program parameters.

2. The community is not in trauma and probably identifies with a reasonably defined geographic area.

3. There is support for project funding over a period of time. This will be based on three expenditure streams:

   a. facilitation team base salaries and running costs

   b. finance for emergent service requirements such as literacy or education programs

   c. finance for emergent capital works or other programs.

4. Time frames have to be long, with realistic expectations of change.

5. Ideally other, larger outside-generated projects and programs will also actively attempt to engage those with a stake in their particular project.

Pragmatically, there needs to be a dedicated suitable on-site office or easy access to something like a hospitable and accessible multipurpose space. The office I had in outback Queensland was good (Figure 6.11). It had a large meeting room, with ample wall space together with two break-out rooms, kitchen and toilets. Nothing flash, but very usable.

Story 24

This might seem a considerable investment, but better that than something only half-considered. While working in an outback town I heard about a series of three-day Future Search conferences that had been run with remote communities. I was told that those held in the town were well received and resulted in a number of groups working on specific projects. However, six months later only one subgroup was still functioning, and that group was chaired by the mayor. My reflection on this is that it is too much to expect a group that is unused to working together to stay the course and actually deliver results. We have to recognise the need for ongoing encouragement and assistance, and not expect instant solutions.

Story 25

Working on a public housing estate, I thought that the logical approach would be to teach a few residents some participatory action research techniques and facilitation fundamentals. How wrong I was. Participatory development is not rocket science – it is far more complex.

There is no doubt in my mind that the key conceptual leap that will underpin the success or failure of the social age is the capacity of those with power (the 'uppers' in any relationship, to use Robert Chambers' language) to consciously use that power to hold the space and enable others to talk to each other and develop their own solutions to complex problems. Without predicting the future, though there is always the potential of foresight, I see a high probability that the effects of climate change will be a catalyst for change to occur. Where this results on the spectrum from manipulation to empowerment of others will be up to those with power in any given situation. To quote Jane Goodall, 'What you do makes a difference and you have to decide what kind of difference you want to make.'

CHAPTER 7

Complexity and our built environment

Writing this book has been akin to the reflection part of the Action Learning cycle. It has been both a reflection of my current practice, and also a method to redefine theory based on that practice. It also sets out my current thoughts on how to best reach the goal as set out by the *Guardian* letter writer in Chapter 1. A significant learning is that to create a plan to achieve the desired outcome is not possible. Because of the nature of working within a complex view of the world to achieve desirable outcomes, it is not possible to plan out a process that is by definition emergent, like fractals (Figure 7.1). Nor is it possible to fantasise or predict what our built cities will look like in 50 or 100 years, because the built environment of the social age will be completely different to that of the technical age. That is the nature of cities and our urban environment generally, both large and small. What is more realistic is to develop and practice an approach to achieving the aim set out by the

Guardian letter writer; that is, a continuous process of Action Learning and reflection with others. The facilitated design process is to support and enable others to develop and grow through a process of transcendental dialogue that achieves agreed decisions. This in turn leads to a stronger social system with such desirable outcomes as resilient and adaptable people and communities, and a culture that values and enhances social capital.

Reality check

This might be a desirable goal, but what if it is in fact, technically, a lost cause? Looking at the planet as rationally as I can, it would seem as if the human species is doing a lot right. More people are alive than ever before, and generally living longer and healthier lives. How good is that? But maybe, just maybe it's too good to last. Maybe we're like so many of those other creatures that simply overbreed and eventually run out of food. Is the situation where we're like lemmings, about to overpopulate and starve ourselves to extinction? Certainly there are many that do predict the apocalypse in all manner of guises, from biblical to scientific.

A critical component in every transition stage of modern cultural development has been the impact of new technology within the system. The printing press revolutionised how new ideas (even musical ones) were conveyed. Later, radio, telephone and film added a new layer of

Figure 7.1 Fractals illustrate a process of change and growth that begin in a small way, building on itself over time.

immediacy and range to communication. It goes without saying that the internet and social media is already having a profound effect on what we call normal, even if our current normal is one of turbulence.

Traditionally, a particular benefit of a city was that it enabled conversation and the exchange of ideas. From the forums of the Greeks through the cathedrals of the medievals, the courts and salons of the gentry, the parliaments of our contemporary society, and the pubs and cafes throughout history, the public space has been the venue for change to be put forward, considered and evaluated. Both conceptually, and to a degree practically, the new digital technology provides a virtual public space that breaks down many of the physical barriers and the tyranny of distance. We can go to the bank, pay our bills, talk with friends, and shout at those we don't like whilst drastically reducing the need for large-scale physical public spaces and travel. To date I have been totally underwhelmed, even exceedingly disappointed, with the type and availability of the digital tools available for genuine collaboration and transcendent conversations. In my experience the architecture of the digital space has been used to either manipulate or dominate others, or crudely further disempower those with less power and reinforce established power holders. Even such useful tools as Google have become a double-edged sword. As a response I have developed a digital workshop venue called The Virtual Centre (Figure 7.2) which would enable real-time workshops such as previously described to occur digitally. I encourage a suitable start-up to build one; I would like to experiment with it. (See https://www.youtube.com/watch?v=1pkyYRs8VbY.) However whilst such technology might be useful, as humans we still exist within the physical realm. And there is no doubt that our collective home is under stress from all manner of forces. Equally there is still the need for both physical connection and physical shelter.

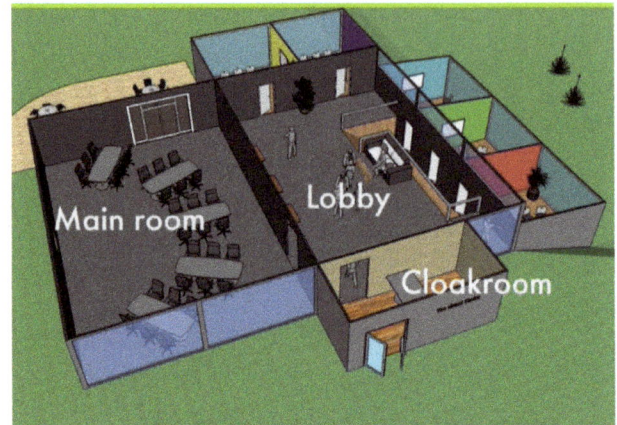

Figure 7.2 The Virtual Centre uses avatars to enable participant engage with each other through workshop processes in real time across geographic boundaries.

As previously mentioned, my inclination is not to predict the future. It is a characteristic of complex systems that they are unpredictable. There is always the potential of catastrophe for the planet, as there is for a 17-year-old with a large motorbike. But there is also the possibility of becoming something completely different to what we are now. How much closer we are to achieving the goal set out by the letter writer will only emerge over time. However to fully embrace the idea of achieving desired outcomes in the social age requires reconsidering what we hold in our minds as an image of a desirable city.

The 'Congrès internationaux d'architecture moderne' (CIAM), in English, International Congresses of Modern Architecture, were hugely influential in directing the thinking behind the modern city. Formed in 1928 (and disbanded in 1959), the members' discussions and manifestos talked of a functionalist city which would embody concepts such as efficiency and effectiveness. The ideal was one of everyone living happy and contented lives through a strategy of creating efficient and technologically sophisticated cities. The manifestation of this strategy was to segregate cities into separate zones for residential, recreational, commercial and industrial activities, all connected by an efficient transport system (like creating a product on a conveyor belt), and buildings were to be technologically efficient machines for living in.

At the time, such ideas of efficiency and effectiveness were part of the industrialist lexicon used in pursuit of producing tangible goods at the most competitive price. A particular goal of designers at the time was to create well-designed artefacts and have them mass produced. In both areas, city and industrial development, the strategy to achieve such efficiencies and effectiveness were from within a technological perspective.

The idea of describing a technological vision for the city can be seen in both formal and less formal drawings of the time. At the formal level are the drawings of Antonio Sant'Elia (Figure 7.3), tragically killed in World War I, Le Corbusier in the 1920s, science fiction style drawings in the 1930s and 1940s (Figure 7.4) with updated versions in the 1960s. An important change in this history of the future is a greater understanding of change and emergence. Thus the science-fiction drawing of the future showed fully complete cities, like a giant building. By 1962 the Japanese architect,

Figure 7.4 Illustration by Frank R. Paul for a science fiction magazine entitled *The City of the Future*, circa 1942.

Arata Isozaki had made a collage (Figure 7.5) to illustrate the transitional and temporary nature of modern cities. But, as can be seen, it is still a conception of a technologically determined city. Given that just as the medieval and Renaissance cities were merely a cultural construct, whether such technologically deterministic visions are relevant in today's period of change is questionable. The data indicates that the modern

Figure 7.3 Drawn in 1914 by Antonio Sant'Elia. Published in *L'architettura futurista: manifesto.*

Cities comprise:
2% of the world's crust
50% of the population
Use 75% of the energy used by the world
Produce 80% of the world's CO2. [1]

Figure 7.5 *Future City (The Incubation Process)*, 1962, photomontage by Arata Isozaki: 'Incubated cities are destined to self-destruct. Ruins are the style of our future cities. Future cities are themselves ruins. Our contemporary cities, for this reason, are destined to live only a fleeting moment...'

city is unsustainable. But is it the only way for people to live?

To be doubly sure that what we currently see as the modern city (and society) is our only option, and not just another cultural construct, I felt it necessary to explore two questions:

1. Are there too many people in the world?

2. Can we grow enough food?

In 1976, after what is often referred to as the first oil crisis of 1973, I attended a lecture by an engineer who had written a book about energy and our use of fossil fuels. This was not long after Pope Paul VI had issued his controversial encyclical (1968) maintaining the Catholic Church's stand on contraception. In the lecture the engineer referred to the calculations used by the Church to assess the possible population that the planet could support. 'But,' he thundered, 'they did not consider the fossil fuels required for modern agricultural practices, and within the next 30 years we will simply run out of fuel to grow sufficient food for everybody.' That was then. The world's population continues to grow and today 50 per cent of food is still produced manually, by women.

More recently, I was on a train with a government scientist responsible for helping farmers work with a changing climate. In answer to my questions about food security in our changing world, he pointed out of the window at what was a rather unremarkable piece of south-eastern Australian countryside. 'Look', he said, 'you ask the average Aussie farmer's opinion of that piece of land, and they'll say you'd struggle to run a couple of goats on it. But if you put a Vietnamese family on there, they'd have it pumping in six months.' He didn't see food security as an issue because in his view food production is a cultural activity. In addition, in his view even with existing technologies the state's arable land is only running at about 50 per cent productivity. And that doesn't even consider such innovations as the suburban fish farm producing organic vegetables in western Sydney. This facility produces five times the amount of food per hectare as traditional farming methods (Figure 7.6).

On another occasion I was walking along the Swan River in Perth with another government scientist, looking across the river to the city. All the high rises were lit up as early evening set in, the city looking every bit the image of the city of the future realised. Out of curiosity I asked her whether it would be technically possible to use some of the farming technologies developed by the marijuana industry to turn the structures into high-rise farms. 'No problem,' was her instant reply. And in fact there are many

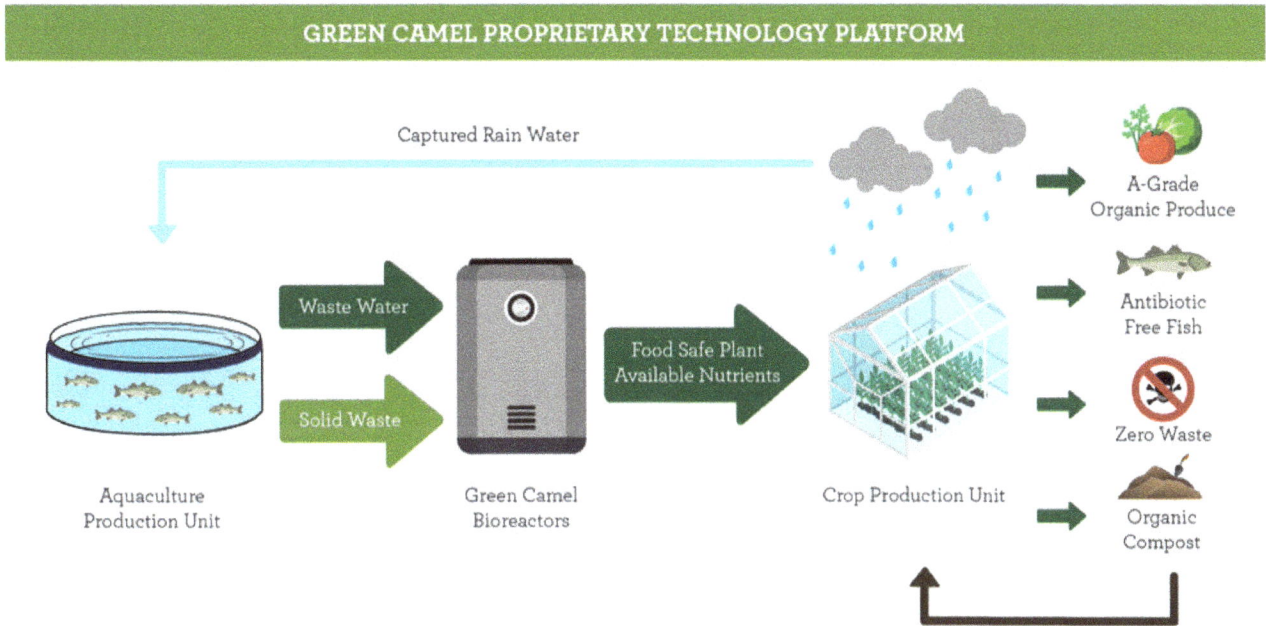

GREEN CAMEL PROPRIETARY TECHNOLOGY PLATFORM

Figure 7.6 The Green Camel enclosed system organic food production plant. Currently supplying high-grade organic food to Sydney supermarkets.

examples of proposals for high-rise farms, both as purpose-built structures or as conversions. It's not a physical limitation as to whether a high-rise tower houses people or pumpkins, it's just where we put the value.

However, maybe that's all still too closely associated with a technologically determined future. So I looked at a couple of books on the subject of urban agriculture. It took me almost no time to find out that the average Australian city could grow 80 per cent of its own nutritional requirements within its own footprint. Again, the issue is not physical limitations. It is just a

matter of whether we want to. Of course, many might object to the idea of growing and eating beans as a major part of everyday life, but that is not something I would propose. It is just an exercise to explore how the limitations to us all having adequate food are not technical, but cultural.

This still leaves the question about the numbers of people in the world, so out of curiosity, I looked at the population density of such highly desirable middle city suburbs as Glen Eira (Melbourne). I found it interesting that at that sort of population density (Figure 7.7) — mainly

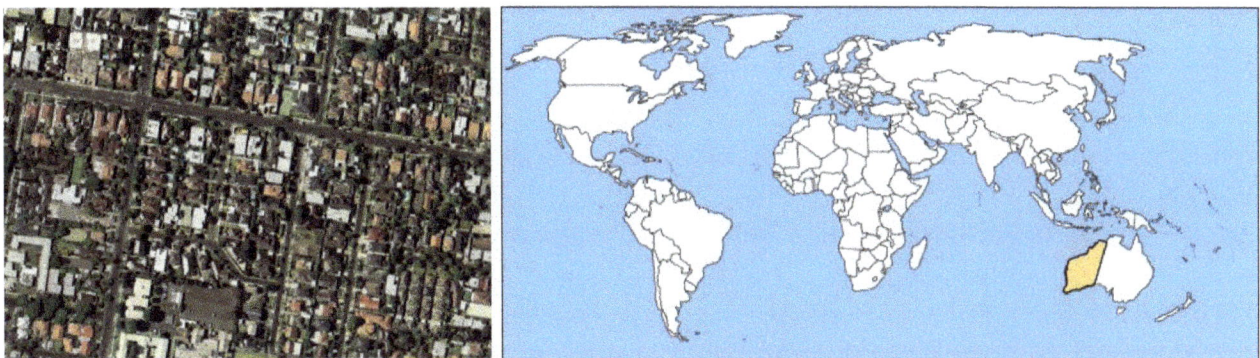

Figure 7.7 At a density of 3,150 people/km2 (the density of Glen Eira, a suburb of Melbourne), everybody in the world would fit into Western Australia.

single-storey suburban houses, some industrial premises, a variety of roads, plenty of parks and open space – the total world population would fit into Western Australia. Of course there are many legitimate reasons as to why it might not be practical for the whole world to live in Western Australia, and I am not proposing it as a way forward. The exercise is just to highlight how with modern technology, there are no longer technical limitations as to where people might live on our planet. Nor is it necessary to all live in high-rise towers just to fit. Limitations of how many people and how to grow enough food are no longer because of insufficient technical knowledge and expertise. It is possible that we will starve to death, but not because of physical or technical limitations but because of how we behave.

To summarise, my extensive and intensive research has convinced me that the end is not nigh for physical reasons. It might be, though, if we don't change our culture, culture being defined as 'the way we do things around here'.

Whilst technology in all its guises will impact the city of the future, the social age will determine its own form. This will be dependent on how well we determine the visions expressed in indeterminate but desirable outcomes.

On a visit to Maputo a few years ago I asked my friend Muchimba what her vision for Maputo would be if it achieved its goal of being developed in 20 years' time. Her answer was: 'Well-built houses, calm, not the noise and stress of developed cities. People with dignity and good health.'

In essence, this is a description of a highly developed social system based on a psychological and social construct. To achieve this will be through actions and outputs based on a different strategic approach to that of today's cities, for the majority of the vision lies outside the realm of solving problems within a complicated system. In other words, what is defined as well-built houses depends on the frame of the individual making the assessment. In consideration of how and where we live (which might be called a city), a first step is to free our imagination about what constitutes the right built solution.

I suspect that we will develop our capacities and capabilities in the social age in much the same way as any of the previous waves of reality. It will be through a continuous process of improvement and innovation. Occasionally there will be startling leaps, but mostly small incremental change, building on the experiences of oneself and others.

Consider the evolution of the car in the technological age. The breakthrough concept was the idea of a horseless carriage. It was then a process of innovation and refinement until achieving the cheap, reliable and ubiquitous products of today. My sense is that on the time scale of the car, our collective consciousness about the nature of complexity, participatory design and social development lies at about 1900. We have some early examples of what it might look like, but most are still thinking about the equivalent of how to make a better horse. The breakthrough concept in the social age is understanding complex systems, and how they work: for example, understanding that Brexit is not a structured innovative approach towards achieving something like the *Guardian* letter writer's ideal, it is more an unintended tipping point in an increasingly unstable period of the world's history.

Just as previous cities were a reflection of the dominant mores of the society that created them, the new and emerging participatory development paradigm will produce a completely different city to anything we've seen before. It may not be a city of tower blocks and freeways, and possibly have only a few odd jetpacks and driverless cars, because the social age will produce something as different to what is the norm today as the technological age is to the theocratic age.

Practically, in thinking about how this might happen, I am reminded of John James's analysis of the innovations in Chartres Cathedral.

Chartres Cathedral is renowned for the number of innovative design and construction details in its fabric. However through a rigorous dating methodology, and a similar analysis of nearby parish churches, James found earlier precedents for every one of the Chartres innovations in the smaller churches. The changes and innovations did not emanate from the big city workshops and then spread out to the regions, but rather the reverse. Innovation occurred at the periphery, and only when successful was it adopted at the centre. In James's words, 'Never practice in front of the Bishop.'

This certainly reflects my own learning story. My sense is that this new way of working – that is, a structured approach to enabling those with a stake in the matters that impact them to be part of solving the problem – will emerge (or are already emerging) from those areas (both physically and administratively) that are not the mainstream, but somewhere considered a bit on the periphery. It might be in some outpost of the developed world, such as outback Australia, or an informal peri-urban area of a developing country's city. Alternatively it might be on the edges of contemporary development practice, such as an innovative council park administrator engaging users and the residents of a street adjacent to a suburban park in how the park might be developed and maintained.

Figure 7.8 The transformation of a disused rail line into a park did not happen through the formal urban planning processes, but through citizen action.

Explorations on the edge

A church mason in the thirteenth century had to have a sufficient understanding of theology, astronomy and numerology to work with the clergy. Designers in the eighteenth century understood the classics, ideas of proportion, the dictates of society, romantic interpretations of the classical empires, and how to represent power and prestige in a pre-technological era. Our professional and technologically driven cities demand technical, problem-solving attributes from its key players. The city of the new paradigm will be the reflection of a society that understands and values human development and social capital. The required skill set will be to design the opportunities for people to work together on the decisions that affect them. It is by working together on real problems that confront us that individuals have the opportunity to practice participatory Action Learning, which in turn provides the opportunities for individual change and growth and a strengthening of the broader system.

The underlying theories for the age of the technical professional were hard science and engineering. It was the CSIRO that developed the ceramic tiles used as a heat shield on the Apollo moon mission. It was the structural engineers at Arup Engineering who worked out how to construct the shells for the Opera House. In the new development paradigm of outcomes it is the psychologists that provide the underlying theory. Maslow was one of the pioneers, describing a hierarchy of people's needs. Since then there has been considerably more research, with further sophistication in understanding such concepts. Compare Maslow's work with the work of Cowen and Beck in Spiral Dynamics. Maslow's Hierarchy of Needs indicates a linear progression from one to another, whilst Spiral Dynamics describes such needs as being in constant flux, spiralling up and down through a progression.

The transformation of a section of 'the El' into an elevated green spine is indeed wonderful (Figure 7.8). This was not a product designed and delivered through the formal development channels, nor was it a scientific and technological feat of expertise. It came about after years of citizen activism. Thus today's challenge focus is not how do we create more elevated parks out of disused railway lines, but how do we enable, encourage and foster the inspiration and vision of everyday people in the topics that matter to them. That the answers and solutions to problems might not be particularly sophisticated, or on the cusp of scientific and social understanding, is not the issue. What will be important is that the solution is 'owned' by those that develop and live with the proposal.

At one time I worked with a colleague to develop and run a course entitled Community Engagement Planning. A segment was to use the Literature Review technique for participants to explore the question 'What is the *essence* of community engagement?' A small experiment I carried out was to keep all the answers to this question. The participants' answers were all based on exactly the same selection of definitions we had mined from the internet. I collected the results of 164 table groups from 54 sessions. In this process, all the table groups considered the same 11 descriptions of the term community engagement, and answered the same final focus question: 'Based on this literature, what does it say is the essence of community engagement?' None of the answers

were the same. None were wrong. However, when looked at more closely, I could see that there was a gradation of sophistication in the answers. Figure 7.9 shows both some of the most and some of the least sophisticated answers.

This spread of sophistication in the answers illustrate a characteristic of complexity in which there are no right or wrong answers to such complex Wicked problems as community engagement, only degrees of better or worse. In this instance, the gradation is one of sophistication in understanding; the degree of sophistication in answers is appropriate to the capacity of those participants – something like the difference in sophistication between the church at Escomb and Salisbury Cathedral.

The difference in today's instance is that viewed from within a complex frame of reality, there needs to be an acceptance that both levels of sophistication (and every one in between) exist at the same time.

Within the city, the built environment can be both the medium and the message, it can express both sophisticated and unsophisticated views of the world. The social age will both acknowledge that to be the case, as well as enabling and assisting people to develop and grow.

Examples of less sophisticated definitions	Examples of more sophisticated definitions
People having a say	A continuous inclusive conversation which addresses issues and achieves outcomes through participation
Valued participation	A group of people continuously collaborating to produce a positive change and a strong sense of belonging
Involvement dialogue	Engagement of all stakeholders in decision making to ensure transparency, access, equity, social justice and accountability
Working together	Brings together people with a common interest to participate in and influence decision making processes with the aim of achieving better outcomes

Figure. 7.9. Examples of sophisticated and unsophisticated answers to the question 'What is the essence of community engagement?'

There are many, many stories of successful collaborative ventures that achieve positive outcomes, and Johns, Kretzman and McKnight document many in *Building Communities from the Inside Out*. I have been fortunate in having two opportunities to specifically influence the traditional capital works procurement process with the explicit intention to strengthen social capital and promote individual growth and change. The first was very simple, but involved promoting a decision that was completely at odds with orthodox concepts of administrative efficiencies and effectiveness.

Strengthening social capital with the built environment

Story 1: The context was in Swaziland when part of the team responsible for constructing 50 houses in a new police camp. The accepted process would have been to have one contractor construct all the houses. To handle such a large project this would have required engaging one of the foreign-based contractors. As an alternative we split the work into five small contracts, each to build 10 houses. This enabled the smaller Swazi building contractors bid for the work. The result was five times as many contracts to administer, but it also provided many desirable outcomes.

We found a healthy combination of competition and collaboration occurred between the contractors. They would pool resources to hire a piece of equipment, but vie with each other to be the first to finish a particular stage. They would watch, share stories and learn from each other. Whilst the rationale we used was risk amelioration, it was the strengthening effect on the social system that was the greatest outcome.

The second was later when working as part of the neighbourhood improvement program for a public housing estate in Australia.

Story 2: A previous study had identified that many residents wanted front fences to the properties. There were 154 houses, and the department allocated funds for about 30 fences in the first year. The officials responsible for allocating the funds were happy that the residents should make the decision as to which houses should first get a fence. We advertised a decision-making workshop open to all residents. At the workshop I ran a Card Storm and ranking process based on the focus question 'Which houses should get a front fence in this round?' (Without making it public, we had broken the sum available for each round into enough for ten fences.) The process elicited a lot of conversations around the definitions of criteria such as being a pensioner, having small children, and being located close to a bus stop. What also emerged was the classification of socially minded, for which the definition provided was that it was those who attend a meeting such as this. This was the criteria that got the most votes, and as there were fewer than ten present, everyone was happy.

Three months later we ran another workshop for the next ten fences, and we got about 15 participants. By the last, we had 30 and whilst not everyone was overjoyed, nobody complained about the allocation. As well as enabling the residents make the decisions, it also meant that the client service officer responsible for the estate was able to keep out of the drama triangle. When a resident demanded to know when they were going to get a fence, the reply was easy: 'It's up to you.'

We subsequently used a variation of the process when money became available to upgrade the houses by building decks, carports, pergolas and performing minor internal works. Whilst this worked well, it was the construction phase that made the most difference to the social fabric of the estate.

The Neighbourhood Job Access Centre was a structured process that enabled individuals from the estate to be awarded mini-contracts to carry out specific pieces of work. It was administratively complicated, and required the skills of a really dedicated builder who understood what we were trying to achieve. Lex, the builder, facilitated the meetings when work was being allocated, and helped and encouraged participants to fulfil their contracts. There is a short YouTube video (https://www.youtube.com/watch?v=uiDUCqSeaXU) on the process and a wider report (Figure 7.10).

A common trope is that the right talks of responsibilities and the left talks of rights. A social approach to development in a complex environment has to stay out of the drama triangle. Complexity demands an understanding that both are required. In this instance we provided the opportunity for people to work in a flexible manner. At the same time, we were not trying to maximise profit or take advantage of their labour. In return they had to carry out the work within the agreed parameters (Figure 7.11).

In the social age, both the bottom-up and top-down approaches will be operating at the same time. And at each step of every development activity different people will see the world through different eyes.

When considering the towns and cities of the social age, what I would like to propose is

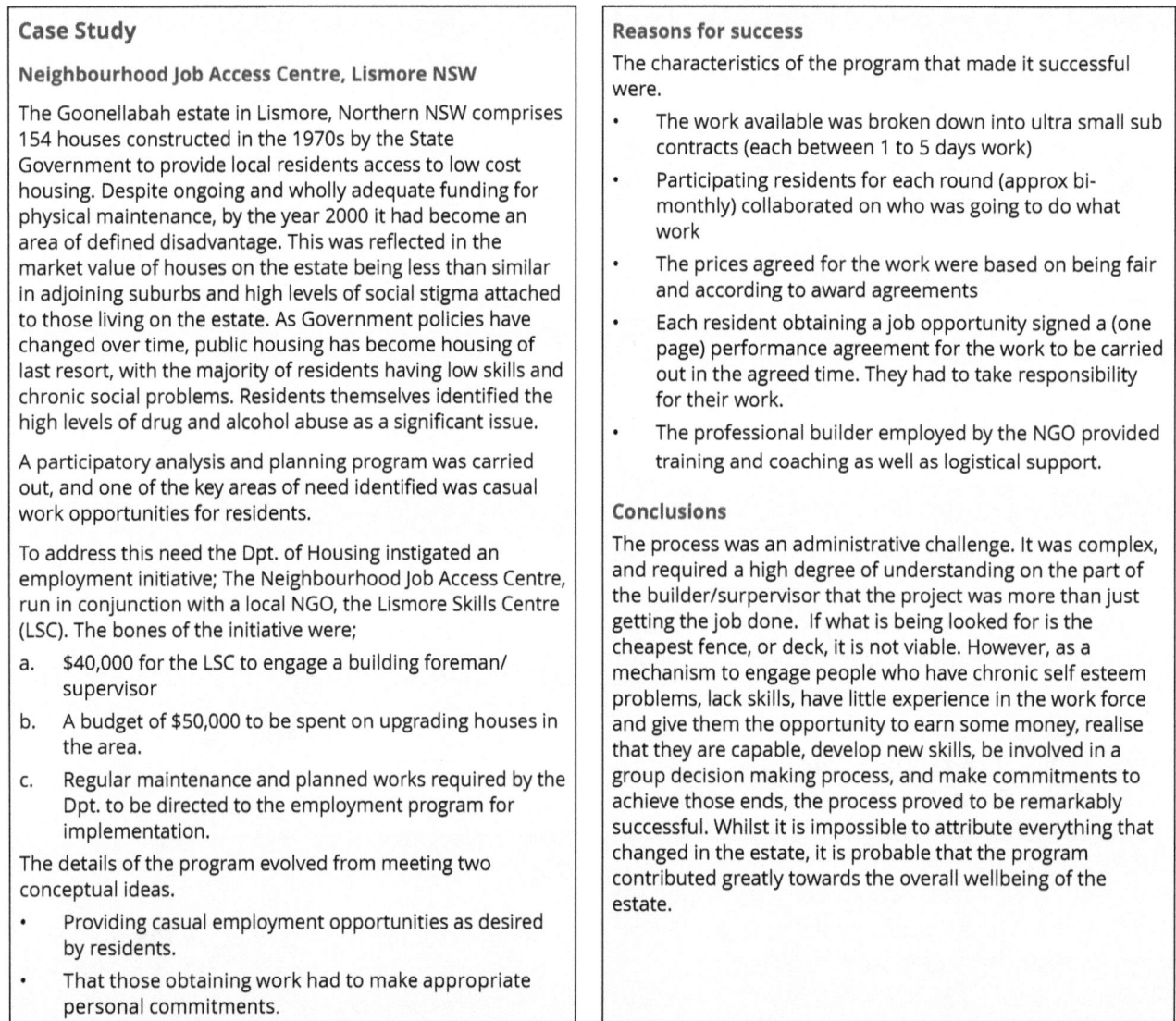

Case Study

Neighbourhood Job Access Centre, Lismore NSW

The Goonellabah estate in Lismore, Northern NSW comprises 154 houses constructed in the 1970s by the State Government to provide local residents access to low cost housing. Despite ongoing and wholly adequate funding for physical maintenance, by the year 2000 it had become an area of defined disadvantage. This was reflected in the market value of houses on the estate being less than similar in adjoining suburbs and high levels of social stigma attached to those living on the estate. As Government policies have changed over time, public housing has become housing of last resort, with the majority of residents having low skills and chronic social problems. Residents themselves identified the high levels of drug and alcohol abuse as a significant issue.

A participatory analysis and planning program was carried out, and one of the key areas of need identified was casual work opportunities for residents.

To address this need the Dpt. of Housing instigated an employment initiative; The Neighbourhood Job Access Centre, run in conjunction with a local NGO, the Lismore Skills Centre (LSC). The bones of the initiative were;

a. $40,000 for the LSC to engage a building foreman/supervisor

b. A budget of $50,000 to be spent on upgrading houses in the area.

c. Regular maintenance and planned works required by the Dpt. to be directed to the employment program for implementation.

The details of the program evolved from meeting two conceptual ideas.

* Providing casual employment opportunities as desired by residents.

* That those obtaining work had to make appropriate personal commitments.

Reasons for success

The characteristics of the program that made it successful were.

* The work available was broken down into ultra small sub contracts (each between 1 to 5 days work)

* Participating residents for each round (approx bi-monthly) collaborated on who was going to do what work

* The prices agreed for the work were based on being fair and according to award agreements

* Each resident obtaining a job opportunity signed a (one page) performance agreement for the work to be carried out in the agreed time. They had to take responsibility for their work.

* The professional builder employed by the NGO provided training and coaching as well as logistical support.

Conclusions

The process was an administrative challenge. It was complex, and required a high degree of understanding on the part of the builder/surpervisor that the project was more than just getting the job done. If what is being looked for is the cheapest fence, or deck, it is not viable. However, as a mechanism to engage people who have chronic self esteem problems, lack skills, have little experience in the work force and give them the opportunity to earn some money, realise that they are capable, develop new skills, be involved in a group decision making process, and make commitments to achieve those ends, the process proved to be remarkably successful. Whilst it is impossible to attribute everything that changed in the estate, it is probable that the program contributed greatly towards the overall wellbeing of the estate.

Figure 7.10 The Neighbourhood Job Access Centre, a social development approach using the built environment.

Figure 7.11 A resident completes her contract to paint a fence whilst babysitting her grandchild.

something modelled on the precepts of a good workshop design. The workshop provides a framework that allows for individuals to express themselves and, in the conversations they have, to develop and grow. The level of sophistication concerning the discussions is not the critical part. What is important is the permission and encouragement for self-expression. By changing the frame from the workshop to the built environment in which the solutions are viewed, possibilities can be seen in a completely different light.

Despite receiving much scorn from some quarters, the suburban environment is a fertile platform for creativity, innovation and personal expression. Almost without exception, it has been the suburban environment that has provided the capacity for individuals to express new ideas, both imaginative and mundane. The newsagents are full of glossy magazines with houses displaying high levels of built sophistication, all of which are essentially within a suburban setting; that is, where individuals have the authority and resources to express their ideas within a defined, agreed and generally accepted set of rules. This provides individuals with the confidence and willingness to commit to quite considerable personal investment. Long may that continue. What I find more interesting is not the sophisticated

buildings in the magazines, but something slightly different.

John Turner wrote *Housing is a Verb* to describe how where we live is more than just a house. The logic or rationale is much the same as Martin Pawley's book *Architecture Versus Housing*. Where, in what kind of living structure, and how we assess it, is absolutely tied up in our everyday life decisions, our education, our lifestyles, aspirations, skills, capacities, hopes and dreams. It is, can be and should be, far more than buying a car or can of beans.

Thus as we move into the social age, the built environment will continue to describe and reflect the kind of society that built it.

A possible indicator of moving in the right direction will be when we see more of the built environment expressing imagination, innovation and the direct expression of diverse world views. The examples in Figure 7.12. might not express great sophistication, but what they do express is the existence of a support system that provides the individuals responsible for them to have felt secure enough, and have had sufficient resources, to express their own ideas about the world and how they fit into it. In the process, they have imagined a different state, made decisions, negotiated and been part of the society that has provided them with this opportunity, carried out a plan and probably learned something along the way. They will have grown and developed both as individuals and contributed to the whole.

As we progress further towards where that perception of the built environment becomes the norm, we will hopefully also be closer to achieving 'a planet where all sentient beings can grow, work, play, create, eat, shit and sleep in perpetuity and safety'.

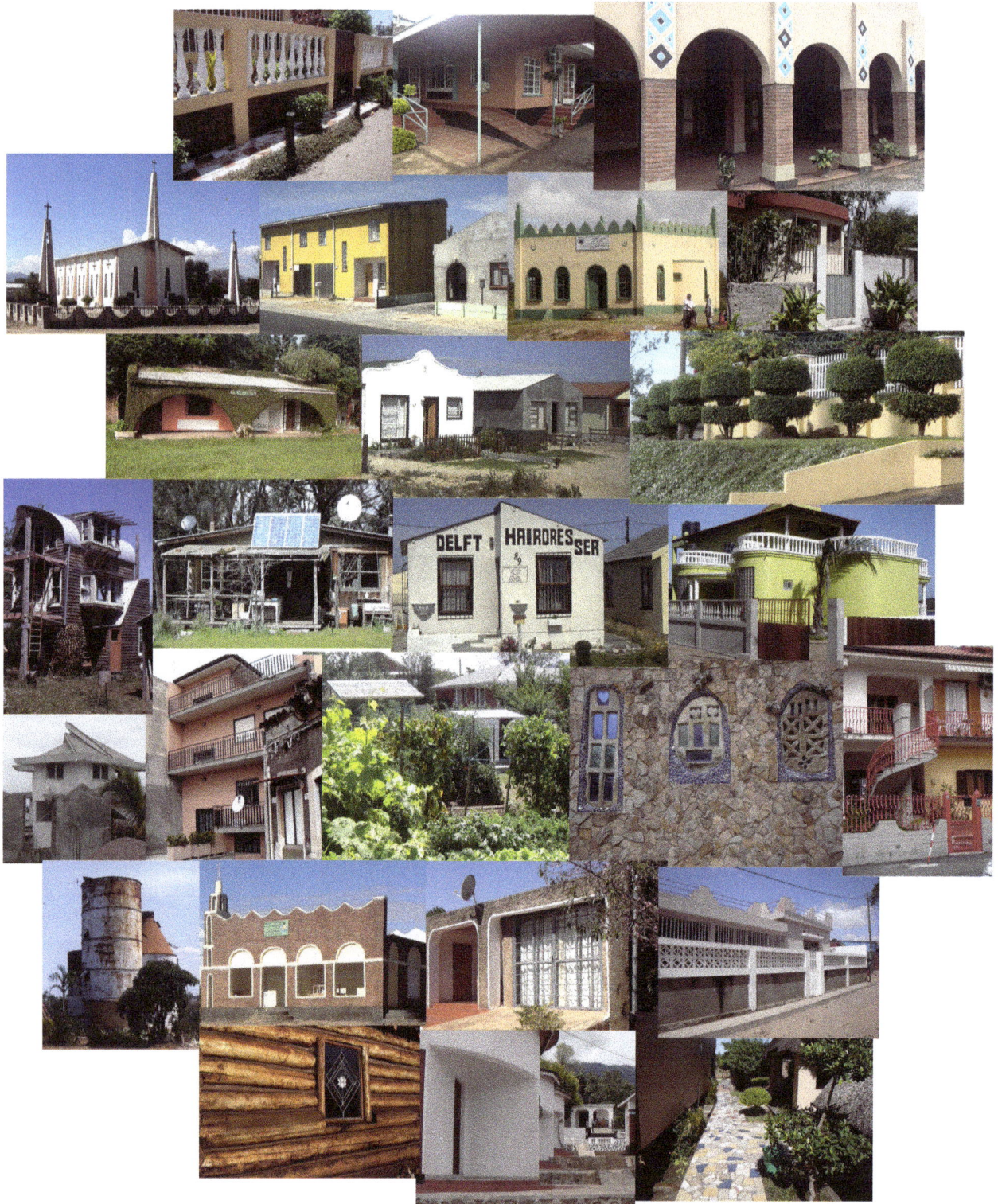

Figure 7.12 There are numerous examples of built structures that might not be particularly sophisticated, but illustrate the potential of people who have access to resources and a sufficient sense of certainty in the system such that they are willing to invest time and effort.

Endnotes

Chapter 1 Setting the stage

1 Culture of change: Umberto Eco, J.-C. C. (2010). *This is not the end of the book*, Harvill Secker.

2 Cultural change: https://en.wikipedia.org/wiki/Culture_change (accessed 17 January 2020)

3 Beechings Axe: http://news.bbc.co.uk/onthisday/hi/witness/march/27/newsid_4339000/4339761.stm (accessed 30 Nov. 2019)

4 Power of the church: Webb, K. (2013). *History NSW Syllabus for the Australian Curriculum Year 8 Stage 4*. Port Melbourne, VIC,

5 Margery Kempe: https://en.wikipedia.org/wiki/Margery_Kempe, (accessed 4 December 2019)

6 Power of the Church: https://www.bl.uk/learning/timeline/item100359.html, (accessed 30 Nov 2019)

7 Seagram Building: Art History, Stokstad and Cothren, 4th edn, p. 1104

8 Wilson's Speech. http://quotes.dictionary.com/the_white_heat_of_the_technological_revolution#uUUjoPyt70oUKGch.99 (accessed 30 Nov 2019)

9 Nikita Khrushchev, http://www.quotationspage.com/quote/25973.html (accessed 23 Jan 2020)

10 Copernicus: https://www.wdl.org/en/item/3164/ Library of Congress; World Digital Library (accessed 19 Jan 2020)

11 Limitations to Power: https://en.wikipedia.org/wiki/English_Civil_War (30 Nov 2019)

12 Gaia: https://en.wikipedia.org/wiki/Gaia_hypothesis (accessed 20 Jan 2020)

13 Vision statement: https://www.changefactory.com.au/our-thinking/articles/the-components-of-a-good-vision-statement/ Accessed 20 Jan 20

14 Enrique Penalosa: (http://quotes.fourthenvironment.com/sources/261, (accessed 13 Dec. 2019).

Chapter 2 The emerging development paradigm

1 Creative leap: https://research.libraries.wsu.edu/xmlui/handle/2376/4163 (accessed 23 Jan 2020)

2 PAR: https://en.wikipedia.org/wiki/Participatory_action_research (accessed 30 Nov 2019)

Chapter 3 Values, power and structure

1 Framing: https://en.wikipedia.org/wiki/Framing_(social_sciences) (accessed 30 Nov 2019)

2 Eco village https://ecovillage.org/about/about-gen/ (accessed 30 Nov 2019)

Chapter 4 Tools and techniques

1 Open Space Technology: https://en.wikipedia.org/wiki/Open_Space_Technology (accessed 30 Nov 20)

Chapter 6 Theory in Use: Reflections and Learning

1 Jane Goodall: https://www.goodreads.com/author/quotes/18163.Jane_Goodall (accessed 20 Jan 2020)

Chapter 7 Complexity and Our Built Environment

1 Cities: https://unhabitat.org/urban-themes (accessed 2 Dec 2019)

Photographs

Photos by the author, except for the following:

1.2 William Hogarth, *The Rake's Progress* (Wikipedia Commons (3 Dec 2019)

1.4 St Swithun's Gate, Winchester, (Sebastian Ballard) https://commons.wikimedia.org/wiki/File:St_Swithun%27s_Gate_-_geograph.org.uk_-_1162914.jpg (3 Dec 2019

1.5 The Gale – artist and provenance unknown. Believed copyright free.

1.6 Bottom Points Lapstone (little Zig Zag) Rail Road NSW 1870 (Courtesy State Library of NSW)

1.7 M1 motorway, (PA Images / Alamy Stock Photo)

1.9 Escomb Church (Hodgsonge) https://commons.wikimedia.org/wiki/File:St_John%27s_Church_,Escomb.jpg

1.10 Salisbury Cathedral (Antony McCallum WyrdLight.com) https://commons.wikimedia.org/wiki/File:SalisburyCathedral-wyrdlight-EastExt.jpg

1.12 Blenheim Palace | iStockphoto 157728843

1.13 Bank Hall (Michael Ely) https://commons.wikimedia.org/wiki/File:Warrington_Town_Hall.jpg

1.15 Isambard Kingdom Brunel (Robert Howlett, 1831–1858)

1.16 Seagram building (http://images.skyscrapercenter.com/building/seagram1_overall_mg.jpg)

1.17 left Cc364 https://commons.wikimedia.org/wiki/File:Cambridge_King%27s_College_Chapel.jpg

1.17 centre United States Capitol (Architect of the Capitol)

1.17 right Gherkin (Aurelien Guichard) https://commons.wikimedia.org/wiki/File:30_St_Mary_Axe_from_Leadenhall_Street.jpg

1.18 An Emirati man riding a camel passes by (KARIM SAHIB Getty Images)

1.20 Cotehele House (Rwendland) https://commons.wikimedia.org/wiki/File:Cotehele,_house_from_courtyard.jpg

https://commons.wikimedia.org/wiki/File:Cotehele,_house_from_courtyard.jpg

1.21 Hampton Court Palace (Luke Nicolaides) https://commons.wikimedia.org/wiki/File:Great_Gate,_Hampton_Court_Palace.jpg

1.22 Hardwick Hall (Chachu207) https://commons.wikimedia.org/wiki/File:Hardwick_Hall_in_Doe_Lea_-_Derbyshire.jpg

1.23 UK Houses of Parliament (http://www.all-free-photos.com/show/showphoto.php?idph=PI67488&lang=en)

1.24 Red House (Ethan Doyle White) https://commons.wikimedia.org/wiki/File:Philip_Webb%27s_Red_House_in_Upton.jpg

1.25 Post Office (public domain) https://en.wikipedia.org/wiki/File:The_Post_Office_in_St_Martin_le_Grand_by_Thomas_Shepherd_(late_1820s).jpg

1.26 https://www.homelessnessaustralia.org.au/about/homelessness-statistics

1.27 Brexit Ian Hinchliffe / Alamy Stock Photo

2.3 a) Cottage: Jonathan Billinger / *Pump Cottage* / CC BY-SA 2.0   b) Redfern,

Sydney–Author c) Nyttend [Public domain] d) Refugee city: Voice of America News: Scott Bobb [Public domain)

2.4   Sydney Opera House Courtesy NSW State Archives: Department of Public Works [II] NRS 12707 "Sydney National Opera House" ("Red Book"), March 1958, p. 1.

4.24   Study Circle (Mark Brophy)

7.1   Fractal (Nelson Charette/Shutterstock)

7.6   Green Camel https://greencamel.com.au/2015/08/23/cloud-based-farming/

7.8   The El https://www.nynjtc.org/sites/default/files/styles/hike_park_destination_page/public/park/highline_0.jpg?itok=sUl-QtBB

Bibliography

Alexander, C. (1965). "The City is Not a Tree." *Architectural Forum* 122(1 & 2): 58-62 (Part I&52).

Arnstein, S. (1969). "A ladder of Citizen Participation." *Journal of the American Planning Association* 35(4): 216-224.

Banham, R. (1960). *Theory and design in the first machine age*, London Architectural Press.

Banham, R. (2009). *Los Angeles - The Architecture of Four Ecologies*. California, University of California Press.

Buck, John and S. Villines (2007). *We The People: Consenting To A Deeper Democracy*, Sociocracy Info Press.

Butcher, M. (2001). "LogFrames made easy." *PLA Notes* IIED PLA 41(June 2001).

Butcher, M. (2006). Community and Stakeholder Engagement Planning. You Tube, https://www.youtube.com/watch?v=1D95bHNgHil – Self published youtube/drmartinbutcher

Butcher, M. (2009) The communication spectrum, Self published https://www.academia.edu/10001527/The_communication_spectrum

Butcher, M. (2010). The Virtual Centre. https://www.youtube.com/watch?v=1pkyYRs8VbY – Self published youtube/drmartinbutcher

Carson, R. (1962.). *Silent Spring*. Cambridge, Mass., Houghton Mifflin Company, Riverside Press.

Chambers, R. (1991). Rapid but Relaxed and Participatory Rural Appraisal: Towards Applications in Health and Nutrition. Rapid Assessment Procedures - Qualitative Methodologies for Planning and Evaluation of Health Related Programs. N. S. Scrimshaw and G. R. Gleason. Boston MA, International Nutrition Foundation for Developing Countries (INFDC). web edition.

Department of Environment Land Water and Planning (DELWP) Community Charter. Melbourne, DELWP.

Dick, B. (1991). *Helping Groups to be Effective*. Chapel Hill, Interchange.

Dick, B. (2001). *Community and organisational change: a manual*. Chapel Hill, Qld, Interchange.

Emery, F. E. and E. L. Trist (1965). "The Causal Texture of Organizational Environments." *Human Relations* 18(1): 21-32.

Jacobs, J. (1992). *The death and life of great American cities* New York Vintage Books.

James, J. (1979). *The Contractors of Chartres*. London, Croom Helm Mandorla Publications.

Kahneman, D. (2011). *Thinking, Fast and Slow*, Macmillan.

Kaner, S. (1996). *Facilitator's Guide to Participatory Decision-Making*. Gabriola Island, New Society Publishers.

Karpman, S. (1968). "Fairy Tales and Script Drama Analysis." *Transactional Analysis Bulletin* 7(26): 39-43.

Kretzmann, J. M. (1993). *Building communities from the inside out*. Chicago, IL, ACTA Publications.

Lazan, G. B. (2000). Global Facilitators Service Corps. 2019.

Lovelock, J. (1988). *The Ages of Gaia: A Biography of Our Living Earth*. New York, W.W. Norton,.

McKie, D. (Tue 3 Nov 2009). The M1 celebrates 50 years. *Guardian*, London.

McLuhan, M. (1967). *The medium is the massage*. UK, Penguin Books.

Meadows, D. H., D. I. Meadows, J. Randers and W. W. Behrens (1972). *The Limits to Growth: a Report for the Club of Rome's Project on the Predicament of Mankind*. New York, Universe Books.

Oliver, P., Ed. (1978). *Shelter and Society: New Studies in Vernacular Architecture*, Vintage.

Orr, D. (1999). An Introduction to the Logframe Approach: Course Workbook and Materials. Melbourne, IDSS Professional Development Program.

Peavey, F. (1994). *By Life's Grace : Musings on the Essence of Social Change*. Philadelphia, New Society Publishers.

Rand, A. (1943.). *The fountainhead*. Indianapolis, Bobbs-Merrill Co.

Rittel+Webber "Dilemmas in a General Theory of Planning." *Policy Science* 4(1973): 155 -169.

Rudofsky, B. (1964). *Architecture Without Architects: A Short Introduction to Non-pedigreed Architecture*. New York, Museum of Modern Art.

Sandman, P. M. "Risk Communication: Facing Public Outrage." *EPA Journal* (U.S. Environmental Protection Agency) 21–22.

Schön, D. (1995). *The Reflective Practitioner*. Aldershot, Ashgate Publishing Ltd.

Schumacher, E. F. (1973). *Small is beautiful: Economics as if people mattered*. New York, Harper & Row.

Snowden, D. "Cynefin Model." 2015.

United Nations (2016). New Urban Agenda. United Nations Conference on Housing and Sustainable Urban Development (Habitat III) Quito Equidor, Habitat III Secretariat.

www.ingramcontent.com/pod-product-compliance
Lightning Source LLC
Chambersburg PA
CBHW051556030426
42334CB00034B/3456